letters to a
young catholic

## Also by George Weigel

*The Courage To Be Catholic: Crisis, Reform, and the Future of the Church*

Tranquillitas Ordinis: *The Present Failure and Future Promise of American Catholic Thought on War and Peace*

*Catholicism and the Renewal of American Democracy*

*American Interests, American Purpose: Moral Reasoning and U.S. Foreign Policy*

*Freedom and Its Discontents: Catholicism Confronts Modernity*

*Just War and the Gulf War* (with James Turner Johnson)

*The Final Revolution: The Resistance Church and the Collapse of Communism*

*Soul of the World: Notes on the Future of Public Catholicism*

*Witness to Hope: The Biography of Pope John Paul II*

*The Truth of Catholicism*

# George Weigel

# letters to a young catholic

BASIC BOOKS
A Member of the Perseus Books Group
New York

Published by Basic Books,
A Member of the Perseus Books Group



Text set in 11 point Janson Text.

Library of Congress Cataloging-in-Publication Data
Weigel, George, 1951–
Letters to a young Catholic / George Weigel.—1st ed.
p. cm.
Includes bibliographical references.
ISBN 0-465-09262-4
1. Catholic youth—Religious life. 2. Weigel, George, 1951—Travel. I. Title.

BX2355.W45 2004
248.4'82—dc22

2003025537

04 05 06 / 10 9 8 7 6 5 4 3 2 1

*To*
*my students in the*
*Tertio Millennio Seminar on the Free Society*
*in Liechtenstein and Kraków,*
*1992–2003*

# Contents

## A Preliminary Postcard

These letters are written to, and for, young Catholics—and not-so-young Catholics, and indeed curious souls of any religious persuasion or none—who wonder what it means to be a Catholic today, at the beginning of the twenty-first century and the third millennium.

There are lots of ways to explore that question. We could take a walk through the *Catechism of the Catholic Church*, reviewing the key points of Christian doctrine and thinking through the myriad challenges of living a Catholic life today. Or we could ponder the lives of the saints, ancient and modern, and see what their experiences have to offer by way of example and inspiration. We could think together about the sacraments of the Church: what does it mean to be baptized, to celebrate the Mass and receive Christ's body and blood in holy communion, to experience the forgiveness of Christ in the sacrament of penance? We could discuss prayer, and its many forms, styles, and methods.

The more I think about it, though, the more it seems to me that the best way to explore the meaning of Catholicism is to take an epistolary tour of the Catholic world, or at least those parts of the Catholic world that have shaped my own understanding of the Church, its people, its teaching, and its way of life. Catholicism is a very tangible business—it's about seeing and hearing, touching, tasting, and smelling as much as it's about texts and arguments and ideas. Visiting some of the more intriguing parts of the Catholic world will, I hope, be an experience of the mystery of the Church, which is crucial to understanding it. And by the "mystery" of the Church, I don't mean the documents long filed away in the Vatican Secret Archives. I mean those dimensions of the Catholic experience that are matters of intuition and empathy and insight—experiences that can never be fully captured discursively.

Where to begin our tour? Perhaps a small autobiographical indulgence isn't out of place in a book like this. So let's begin by visiting the Catholic world of my youth. At the very least, it's an interesting slice of Americana. I think it's more than that, though. When I was a very young Catholic, I absorbed things by a kind of osmosis, things that just may shed light on the fuller and deeper truths of Catholic faith today—even though we're living in a very different time and place and circumstance.

# letters to a young catholic

# 1

# Baltimore and Milledgeville— Acquiring the "Habit of Being"

I grew up in seemingly the last moment of intact Catholic culture in the United States: the late 1950s and early 1960s in Baltimore, one of the most Catholic cities in the country. There were lots of places like this—Boston, surely; large parts of New York and Philadelphia; Chicago and Milwaukee and St. Louis. Still, there was something distinctive about Catholic Baltimore in those days. American Catholics past and present are notoriously ignorant of the history of the Church in the United States. In Baltimore, we were very much aware that we were living in the first of American dioceses, with the first bishop and the first cathedral—and, of course, the *Baltimore Catechism*, which was used in those days from sea to shining sea.

Catholic Baltimore was different from other parts of America's urban Catholic culture in degree, not in kind. We didn't divide the world into "Baltimore Catholicism" and "Milwaukee Catholicism" (or Philadelphia Catholicism, or New York Catholicism, or Boston Catholicism, or whatever). We quite naturally and unself-consciously divided the world into "Catholics"—people we recognized by a kind of instinct—and "non-Catholics." That instinct wasn't a matter of prejudice. It was the product of a unique experience, and you instinctively recognized people who'd been formed by the same experience.

How were we different? To begin with, we had a singular way of describing ourselves. When someone asked us where we were from, we didn't say South Baltimore or Highlandtown or Towson or Catonsville. We'd say "I'm from Star of the Sea" (or St. Elizabeth's or Immaculate Conception or St. Agnes, or, in my case, the New Cathedral). Baltimore was (and is) a city of neighborhoods, but in hindsight it seems instructive that we identified ourselves first by parish rather than geographic area. Some might call this "tribal," and there were certainly elements of the tribal (especially ethnic tribal) in this distinctive way of telling a stranger who you were. It was a different kind of tribalism, though, a *Catholic* tribalism that fostered fierce rivalries and even fiercer loyalties: rivalries among parishes and schools and teams and youth groups, but beyond and through all those rivalries, an intense sense of belonging to something larger than ourselves, something beyond ourselves that somehow lived inside us, too. All of which was, as I look back on it, a first inkling of "catholicity" (which is another word for "universality") and its relationship to particularity.

We used a different vocabulary in the Catholic world in which I grew up. With the possible exception of grinds aiming to score 800 on the SAT verbals, the only American kids between the ages of ten and eighteen who regularly used words like vocation, monstrance, missal, crucifer, biretta, chasuble, surplice, ciborium, and paten were Catholics. (This arcane, Latin-derived vocabulary was a source of aggravation to generations of high school and college English composition teachers, eager to get us using short, sharp words of Anglo-Saxon origin rather than those luxurious Latinate nouns and verbs.) We also pronounced words differently: non-Catholics said "Saint AW-gus-teen," but we knew it was "Saint Uh-GUS-tin." Then there was our sense of identification with some local heroes. Other kids could recite the relevant batting and pitching, passing and receiving statistics of their sports idols, but hadn't a clue (and couldn't have cared less) about their religious affiliation. We were stat crazy, too, but we also knew who the Catholics were (John Unitas, Artie Donovan, Brooks Robinson) and what parish they belonged to. And we sensed a connection to these athletic gods that was . . . different, somehow.

With our Catholic school uniforms, we looked different—and if those uniforms saved our parents a lot of clothes money (which they did), they also reinforced a sense of belonging to something distinctive. So did the fact that we were taught by religious sisters (whom we mistakenly called "nuns," ignorant of the canonical technicality that "nuns" are, by definition, cloistered). Some were magnificent: my first-grade teacher, Sister Mary Moira, S.S.N.D., understood "phonics" a generation ahead of time and could teach a stone to read. Others were, to put it gently, less than adequate: my seventy-something fifth-grade teacher, Sister Maurelia, still insisted that the sun orbited the earth. Yet even the bad teachers commanded respect, and through the combined effects of their personal discipline, austerity, and devotional lives, even the bad teachers were teaching us something important about life and its purposes, however clumsily or inarticulately. (And yes, there were occasional Ingrid Bergman/*Going My Way* moments: Sister

Maurelia's devotion to the Ptolemaic universe coexisted with an impressive capacity to clobber a misbehaving boy with a well-aimed chalkboard eraser at twenty paces. Anyone who described such behavior as "abusive" would have been considered insane.)

Our calendar, and the habits it bred into us, also marked us out as distinctive. "Holy days" (like the December 8 feast of Mary's Immaculate Conception) were days off from school—a source of envy among the "publics," as we sometimes called the kids in the government schools. In that innocent era, before Christian terminology in the government schools was deemed a danger to the Republic, everybody had "Christmas vacation." But we had "Easter vacation" while everybody else had "spring break." Meatless Fridays set us apart from our non-Catholic friends and neighbors: no one else we knew took peanut butter and jelly (or tuna fish or Swiss cheese on rye) sandwiches to school in their lunch bags (or lunch boxes, among the smaller fry). Our parents couldn't eat meat at breakfast and lunch on the weekdays of Lent, and everyone fasted for three hours before going to church on Sunday morning. First Communion (in the second grade) and Confirmation (in the fourth grade) were major landmarks in our uniquely Catholic life cycle.

Our Protestant friends knew their Bible a lot better than we did, but we knew our catechism. Looking back, I see that the memorization of its answers was not only the basic structure of our early religious instruction—it was a first hint that Catholicism is deeply, even passionately, invested in ideas, even ideas boiled down into single-sentence formulas. (Little did we know the titanic struggles that had gone into creating those precise formulations over the centuries.) We had a ritual life that also set us apart. Most of us went to Mass every Sunday (plus those blessed, school-free holy days), and the idea of a churchless Sunday struck us as somehow odd. The Mass was, of course, celebrated in Latin (with the Gospel read in English before the sermon). Catholic boys memorized "the responses" in Latin in order to serve at the altar (the frequent response *Et cum spiritu tuo* giving rise, phonetically, to the old saw about the classic Catholic telephone number: "Et cum speery, two-two-oh"). From constant repetition during Benediction of the Blessed Sacrament and from the weekly Lenten devotion known as the Stations of the Cross, boys and girls alike learned a few Latin hymns ("Tantum ergo," "O salutaris hostia," "Stabat mater"). And for some reason, perhaps best understood by religious anthropologists, it didn't strike us as the least bit peculiar that we prayed and sang in an ancient language that few of us knew—until, that is, Latin was drummed into us, declension by declension and conjugation by conjugation, when we hit high school.

Some of the things we did raised the eyebrows of our more assertively Protestant neighbors. Our piety had a distinctly Marian flavor, unintelligible and perhaps vaguely blasphemous to non-Catholics. Catholic families were frequently encouraged to say the rosary together, and the annual "May procession" was a great event on the school and parish calendar; its high point came when an especially favored girl from the parish school "crowned" a statue of Mary with a garland of flowers. What truly marked us off as different, though (in the eyes of some, perversely different), was what everyone in those days called "going to confession." Making one's first confession was an absolute and unchallenged prerequisite to First Communion. So, at age seven or eight we learned an etiquette of self-examination and self-accusation that our Protestant friends (when they got up the nerve to ask) found incomprehensible. Mythologies notwithstanding, "going to confession" wasn't a terrifying or morbid experience: at least once a month we were taken to church from the parochial school and lined up outside the confessional to do our penitential duty, about which, insofar as I can recall, no one complained. All of this (examining conscience, making a "firm purpose of amendment," describing our peccadilloes, receiving and saying a brief penance) was simply what we did because of who we were. If other people didn't do such things, they were the odd ducks, not us. They were the ones missing something.

Then there were our international connections, which seemed more richly textured than our neighbors'. American Christians have always been mission conscious. Still, I don't recall hearing my Protestant friends talk about "ransoming pagan babies," which was something we did during Lent throughout my early years in elementary school. In those days, when a quarter was a lot of money, the idea was to put your pennies and nickels in a small cardboard collection box you kept at home. Over the forty days of Lent the goal was to collect a total of five dollars—which required another form of self-discipline: not raiding the collection box too often. This five dollars would be given to a mission, usually in Africa, and in return, the donor was allowed to give the "pagan baby" its Christian name at its baptism (if memory serves, we got a certificate noting that "James" or "Mary" had been baptized because of our generosity). I never quite figured out how this worked at the other end, unless all our "pagan babies" were orphans without parents to name them. The point, however, was not the logistics, but the sense that was quickly ingrained in us of being part of a worldwide body. Mission talks were a regular feature of Catholic schools, and the Catholic periodical literature of the day (even for children) was chock-full of stories from the missions, some bloodcurdling. The Jesuits and the Religious of the Sacred Heart may have been the up-market religious orders when I was growing up, but the Catholic Foreign Mission Society of America—Maryknoll—was where the adventure was. Few Catholic youngsters didn't dream, at least briefly, of becoming a missionary, and even a missionary martyr.

We were also aware of belonging to a worldwide Church that was under serious persecution in various places. The idea of a "Christian–Marxist dialogue" was buried in the womb of the future. What we knew about communism was that communists had killed Yugoslavia's Cardinal Stepinac, tortured Hungary's Cardinal Mindszenty, and locked up the gentle Bishop James Edward Walsh of Maryknoll (a fellow Marylander and veteran China missionary). Some of this storytelling had an effect on me that I couldn't imagine at the time.

A lot of my writing over the past twenty-five years has had to do with Poland, and I can't help but think that the seeds of my Polish passion were planted early—in the third grade, to be precise. In early 1959, the principal of the Old Cathedral School in downtown Baltimore, Sister Euphemia, announced that each class in the school would be assigned a communist dictator for whose conversion we were to pray during Lent. Everybody wanted Nikita Khrushchev, of course, because he was the only communist dictator most of us had ever heard of. So there was great disappointment in the third grade when, by the luck of the draw, we got the chief Polish communist, Władysław Gomułka. More than thirty years later I would write a book that, among other things, chronicled Gomułka's complex role in Polish Church–state relations; you can't tell me there isn't a connection, somehow, to that third-grade experience.

The other great international linkage that made us different was, of course, the link to what an earlier generation of anti-Catholics bigots (in our grandparents' time) had called a "foreign potentate"—the pope. The sense of connection to "Rome" and to the pope himself was strong. Pius XII, the pope of my boyhood, was an ethereal figure; yet every Catholic I knew seemed to feel a personal attachment to him, and I well remember the tears shed when he died in October 1958. I was in the second grade and, along with all eight grades of the Old Cathedral School, marched across Mulberry Street into the Cathedral of the Assumption, where one of the young priests on the cathedral staff led us in five decades of the rosary. Our elders, for the next few days, said that "there would never be another pope like Pius XII" (a good call, if not for the reasons they imagined at the time). When a portly, seventy-seven-year-old Italian named Roncalli was elected and took what sounded like a bizarre name, "John XXIII," those same elders sagely noted that things just weren't the same (they got that right, too, if again for an entirely different set of reasons). This emotional and spiritual connection to the bishop of Rome never seemed to us odd, much less un-American, and the anti-Catholic agitation of the 1960 presidential campaign struck us as weird rather than threatening. We knew we were Catholics *and* Americans, and if someone else had a problem with that, well, that was, as we used to say, *their* problem. It certainly wasn't ours.

So we were . . . different, and we knew ourselves to be different, yet without experiencing ourselves as strangers in a strange land. Garry Wills and I haven't agreed on much recently, but Garry had it exactly right in an elegiac essay written in the early 1970s, when he said that our generation of Catholics in America had grown up in a ghetto—just as he was right when he also wrote that it wasn't such a bad ghetto in which to grow up. Indeed, the most ghettoized people of all, I've come to learn, are those who don't know they grew up in a particular time and place and culture, and who think they can get to universal truths outside of particular realities and commitments. There are ghettos and then there are ghettos. The real question is not whether you grow up in a ghetto, but whether the ideas and customs and rhythms of your particular ghetto prepare you to engage other ideas and customs and life experiences without losing touch with your roots. Long before Alex Haley successfully marketed the idea, the importance of "roots" was drummed into us because without roots there's no growth, only dryness and decay.

---

Whether we knew it or not (and most of us didn't or didn't know until later in life), this "Catholic difference" wasn't only a matter of how we described ourselves, how we talked, what we wore and ate, where we went to school, and who taught us. The real "Catholic difference"—which was mediated to us by all these other differences—was, at bottom, a way of seeing the world.

And, by a roundabout route, this brings us to the first proposition I'd like you to consider: while Catholicism is a body of beliefs and a way of life, *Catholicism is also an optic, a way of seeing things, a distinctive perception of reality.*

What is it? You can describe it in many ways. You can call it the "Catholic both/and": nature *and* grace, faith *and* works, Jerusalem *and* Athens, faith *and* reason, charismatic *and* institutional, visible *and* invisible. You can call it the "sacramental imagination" (about which, much more later). You can call it a taste for the analogical, as distinguished from some Protestants' taste for the dialectical. You can, in the broadest terms, call it "Catholic culture." However it's described, though, it's not something you simply argue yourself into. Rather, it's something you experience aesthetically as well as intellectually, with the emotions as well as the mind, through friendships and worship and experiences-beyond-words as well as through arguments and syllogisms. And that, to go back to the beginning, is why, in thinking through the question of what it means to be a Catholic today, it's a good idea to make a tour of the Catholic world—because there are particular places where this uniquely Catholic way of seeing things comes into clearer focus.

Which brings us to another, perhaps unlikely, place at the beginning of our journey: Milledgeville, Georgia, deep in the heart of Dixie, the least Catholic part of the United States—demographically speaking, at least.

Andalusia Farm outside Milledgeville was the home of Flannery O'Connor, one of the most remarkably gifted American writers of the past half century. F. Scott Fitzgerald, another great mid-twentieth-century writer, couldn't escape his boyhood Catholicism, no matter how hard he tried (and he tried *very* hard). Flannery O'Connor wrote the way she did precisely because she was a dead-serious Catholic with a deep intuition about the Catholic optic on life.

Born in Savannah in 1925, Mary Flannery O'Connor and her family moved to Andalusia Farm when she was twelve. In 1945 she graduated from the Georgia State College for Women, and then studied at the famous Writers' Workshop at the University of Iowa. In 1949 the onset of lupus, the disease that had taken her father's life before Flannery was sixteen, brought her home to Milledgeville, where she spent the rest of her life (save for the occasional out-of-town lecture), and where she died in 1964, at thirty-nine.

Her writing habits were as austere as her prose: her desk faced a whitewashed wall, and she wrote her fiction looking at that blank space. What she wanted to convey in her stories and novels came out of her head and her reading and her reflection and her prayer; and what she wrote was often misunderstood as dark parody and violent satire, when in fact she was holding up a mirror to a modern world that had come to think of its distortions as natural (as she once put it). Fifteen years after her death, her friend Sally Fitzgerald edited and published a collection of her letters under the title, *The Habit of Being*. And the world discovered a new Flannery O'Connor—a gifted Catholic apologist and razor-sharp analyst of the "Catholic difference" in its sometimes challenging, sometimes enthusiastic, and always bracing encounter with modern culture.

Flannery O'Connor's novels and short stories struck her first critics, and often strike readers today, as being dominated by grotesques. (Asked why she wrote so frequently about grotesques, Miss O'Connor, who had a very dry wit, used to reply that, in the South, they liked to think they could still recognize them.) In fact, Flannery O'Connor's fiction is pervaded by a deeply Catholic intuition about the temper of our times and what the peculiarly modern determination to identify freedom with radical personal autonomy—"my way"—has done to us. As she put it in one of those posthumously published letters (referring to a "moronic" review of one of her stories in the *New Yorker*), "the moral sense has been bred out of certain sections of the population, like the wings that have been bred off certain chickens to produce more white meat on them." By "moral sense," I think Miss O'Connor meant the "habit of being," that spiritual sensibility which allows us to experience the world, not as one damn thing after another but as the dramatic arena of creation, sin, redemption, and sanctification. "This is a generation of wingless chickens," O'Connor continued, "which is I suppose what Nietzsche meant when he said God is dead." The proclamation of the death of God had resulted in the death of the truly human: what was left behind were wingless chickens.

And here's the second proposition to ponder: for all the sentimentality that occasionally clings to Catholic piety, *there is nothing sentimental about Catholicism.* "There is nothing harder or less sentimental than Christian realism," Flannery O'Connor wrote, because Christianity stands or falls with the incarnation—God's entry into history through Jesus of Nazareth, who is both the Son of God, the Second Person of the Trinity, and the son of Mary, a young Jewish girl living on the outer fringes of the Roman Empire. History and humanity are the vehicles by which God reveals himself to the world he created. History is the arena, and humanity the vessel, through which God redeems the world. History and humanity *count*, and count ultimately: not because of our pride but because of God's merciful love, the unsentimental but cleansing love of the father who welcomes the prodigal son home, knowing full well that the prodigal has made a thoroughgoing mess of his life by his selfishness, his "autonomy," his conviction that nothing, including himself, really counts.

"If you live today, you breathe in nihilism . . . it's the gas you breathe," wrote Flannery O'Connor; "if I hadn't had the Church to fight it with or to tell me the necessity of fighting it, I would be the stinkingest logical positivist you ever saw right now." So, I expect, would I. So, perhaps, would you. So here's one more way to think about Catholicism and its distinctive optic on the world and on us: *Catholicism is an antidote to nihilism*. And by "nihilism," I mean, not the sour, dark, often violent nihilism of Nietzsche and Sartre, but what my friend, the late Father Ernest Fortin (who borrowed the term from his friend, Alan Bloom), used to call "debonair nihilism": the nihilism that enjoys itself on the way to oblivion, convinced that all of this—the world, us, relationships, sex, beauty, history—is really just a cosmic joke. Against the nihilist claim that nothing is really of consequence, Catholicism insists that *everything* is of consequence, because everything has been redeemed by Christ.

And if you believe that, it changes the way you see things. It changes the way *everything* looks. Here is Flannery O'Connor again, reflecting on the Catholic difference in her own artistic and spiritual life, and that of fellow author Caroline Gordon Tate:

> *I feel that if I were not a Catholic, I would have no reason to write, no reason to see, no reason ever to feel horrified or even to enjoy anything. I am a born Catholic, went to Catholic schools in my early years, and have never left or wanted to leave the Church. I have never had the sense that being a Catholic is a limit to the freedom of the writer, but just the reverse. Mrs. Tate told me that after she became a Catholic, she felt she could use her eyes and accept what she saw for the first time, she didn't have to make a new universe for each book but could take the one she found.*

To be sure, Catholicism wants to change the world—primarily by converting it. At the same time, Catholicism takes the world as it is—Catholicism tries to convert *this* world, not some other world or some other humanity of our imagining—because God took the world as it is. God didn't create a different world to redeem; God, in the person of his Son, redeemed the world he had created, which is a world of freedom in which our decisions have real consequences, for good and for evil. Flannery O'Connor used to complain, wryly, that the critics who described her fiction as "horror stories" always had "hold of the wrong horror." The horror isn't wickedness. The horror of the modern world is that, if nothing is really of ultimate consequence, then the wickedness isn't really wicked, the good isn't good, and we're back, once again, to all those pathetic "wingless chickens."

Flannery O'Connor's wry wit may be giving you the impression that being Catholic and being feisty are not mutually exclusive. Good. Let's ratchet that up a notch. In the late 1940s, Miss O'Connor, then an aspiring young writer, was taken to a literary dinner in New York at the home of Mary McCarthy, who had made a considerable success out of the story of her break from the Church. Invitations to dinner with Mary McCarthy, a certified literary heavyweight on the New York scene, were gold and frankincense to struggling writers; Flannery O'Connor played the evening rather differently than your typical fledgling author-on-the-make. Here's her description of the self-consciously sophisticated repartee of that dinner party, and her sole contribution to it:

> *I was once . . . taken by some friends to have dinner with Mary McCarthy and her husband, Mr. Broadwater. (She just wrote that book,* A Charmed Life.*) She departed the Church at the age of 15 and is a Big Intellectual. We went at eight and at one, I hadn't opened my mouth once, there being nothing for me in such company to say. The people who took me were Robert Lowell and his now wife, Elizabeth Hardwick. Having me there was like having a dog present who had been trained to say a few words but overcome with inadequacy had forgotten them. Well, toward morning the conversation turned on the Eucharist, which I, being the Catholic, was obviously supposed to defend. Mrs. Broadwater said when she was a child and received the Host, she thought of it as the Holy Ghost, He being the "most portable" person of the Trinity; now she thought of it as a symbol and implied that it was a pretty good one. I then said, in a*

> *very shaky voice, "Well, if it's a symbol, to hell with it." That was all the defense I was capable of but I realize now that this is all I will ever be able to say about it, outside a story, except that it is the center of existence for me; all the rest of life is expendable.*

Now, there's a lot to be learned from modern philosophy and theology about the difference between a "sign" (which simply conveys a message, like "Stop" or "This is Crest toothpaste") and a "symbol," a more complex reality that makes present, or embodies, the truth it communicates (a wedding ring, for instance). And yes, there's a certain theological sense in which the sacraments are "symbols" through which Christ is really and truly present to his people, the Church. But prior to such distinctions, important as they are, is the gut *Catholic* instinct that Flannery O'Connor defended so rashly in Mary McCarthy's living room. If Mary McCarthy was right, and the Eucharist only represented Christ in some magical way, then Flannery O'Connor was being utterly, thoroughly, radically orthodox when she muttered, "Well, if it's a symbol, to hell with it."

The Catholic imagination, this *habit of being* we've been exploring, is serious business. An evangelical Protestant of my acquaintance once said to a Catholic friend, "If I really believed, like you say you do, that Christ himself is in that tabernacle, I'd be crawling up the aisle on my hands and knees." That's about half right, for the Catholic habit of being teaches us both the fear of the Lord (in the sense of being awestruck by the majesty and mercy of God) and an intimacy, even familiarity, with God the Holy Trinity, through the personal relationship with Jesus Christ that is the heart of Catholic faith. Inside that distinctively Catholic "both/and" of the intimate and the awesome lies the conviction that *all of this is for real.* Stuff counts. I count. You count. It all counts. Because all of it—you, me, our friends, our critics, the man I jostled on the subway this morning and the bag lady sleeping on the heating grate at the Farragut North metro stop, the whole mad, sad, noble, degraded, endlessly fascinating human story—is really His-story, Christ's story, supercharged with that fullness of truth and love that can only come from Truth and Love itself: that can only come from God.

---

That's what I learned, at least in terms of instincts, in those last years of the intact urban Catholic culture of America. I learned what Flannery O'Connor later named for me as the "habit of being." For all its gaudiness, the world of debonair nihilism in which you've grown up sees the world in black-and-white, and in two dimensions only. In the world of debonair nihilism, there is only me, and there are only transient pleasures to be grasped and indulged and then quickly forgotten, on the way to the next ephemeral high produced by my willfulness. By contrast, the Catholic imagination, this habit of being, teaches us to see the world in Technicolor and to live in it in three dimensions (or, truth to tell, four, because time counts, too, for Catholicism as well as for Einstein).

That's the habit I hope this correspondence and our tour of the Catholic world helps you acquire: the habit of being, the habit of seeing things in depth, as they are and for what they are. Everything that is, is for a reason. Everything that happens, happens for a purpose. That's what it means to understand history as His-story. Seeing things in their true dimensions is one very large part of what it means to be a Catholic. For learning to see things aright *here* is how we become the kind of people who can see, and love, God forever.

# 2

## Rome—The *Scavi* of St. Peter's and the Grittiness of Catholicism

Pope Pius XI died on February 10, 1939. Prior to his election as bishop of Rome in 1922, he had been the archbishop of Milan for a brief period, and the Milanese wanted to honor his memory by building a fitting resting place for him in St. Peter's Basilica. So funds were raised, artists commissioned, and a magnificent marble sarcophagus, which was to be the centerpiece of a richly decorated mosaic vault, was prepared and sent to Rome.

According to one story I've heard, when it came time to fit the new tomb into the grottoes underneath the papal high altar in St. Peter's, it was simply too large. Perhaps that's a case of historical embellishment, which isn't rare in Italy; or perhaps it's just a typical Roman attempt to tweak the usually efficient Milanese. In any event, there were longstanding plans to renovate the entire grotto area and make it a more appropriate place for pilgrims to pray. So Pope Pius XII, successor to Pius XI, ordered the floor of the undercroft to be lowered to make room for the tomb of his predecessor and to take a first step in the planned renovation.

It was a decision with unforeseen consequences.

What we know today as St. Peter's used to be called New St. Peter's to distinguish it from Old St. Peter's, the basilica built by the Emperor Constantine in the fourth century, over what he and everyone else understood to be the grave of Peter, prince of the apostles. Despite his absorption in planning the new imperial capital at Constantinople, Constantine helped with the construction of his magnificent St. Peter's by carrying twelve baskets of earth to the site, one for each of the twelve apostles. For more than a millennium, Old St. Peter's was one of the focal points of the Christian world, a pole toward which Christians' internal compasses naturally pointed.

By the second half of the fifteenth century, however, Old St. Peter's had fallen to rack and ruin; the decision was made to pull it down to make way for a new basilica. The building of New St. Peter's, which would eventually include the world's largest dome and the fantastically strong foundations needed to support it, took 120 years and absorbed the attention of twenty popes and ten architects, including such legends as Bramante, Michelangelo, and Bernini. The building's changing design, the execution of those designs, and the fund-raising necessary to support such a vast project caused a lot of controversy, and contributed in at least an indirect way to the Reformation. Amid all the confusion and construction, little was done to explore the tomb of St. Peter. It was simply assumed to be where tradition and Constantine had sited it. "New St. Peter's" was thus built without any systematic excavation of what was underneath Old St. Peter's.

When the workmen began lowering the floor of the undercroft to accommodate the tomb of Pope Pius XI and renovate the grotto space, they discovered a series of tombs that, on further examination, seemed to be part of a kind of necropolis, complete with walls, streets, benches, funerary monuments, and so forth. Much of this had been disturbed or destroyed when the ancient Vatican Hill was leveled by Constantine's fourth-century builders, but a fair amount of it was still intact. While World War II raged across Europe, Pius XII quietly authorized a full-scale archaeological excavation of the area, which continued throughout the 1940s.

Digging under the papal high altar of the basilica was something like peeling an onion or opening one of those nested Russian *matrushka* dolls. Eventually the excavators found a shrine, the Tropaion (the Greek word for trophy or victory monument): a classic structure, with columns supporting what may have been an altar, surmounted by a pediment. The floor of the Tropaion, which has an opening delineating the boundaries of the grave over which the monument was built, defined the level of the floor of Constantine's basilica. At the back of the Tropaion was a red wall; exposed to the elements, it began to crack, necessitating the construction of a buttressing wall to support the whole structure. When archaeologists unearthed the buttressing wall, they found it covered with graffiti. And it contained a secret, marble-lined repository. One piece of graffiti, decoded, seemed to say, "Peter is [here]"

Thanks to long delayed renovation plans, the need to accommodate Pius XI's tomb, and the curiosity of Pius XII (who seems to have been intrigued by the discovery of King Tut's tomb in 1923), archaeologists eventually unearthed a small city of the dead beneath the foundations of Old St. Peter's, which had been incorporated into New St. Peter's as supports for the colossal new structure. There had been, evidently, a vast pagan burial ground on the Vatican Hill. At some point, Christians began to be buried there. The central grave that defines the Tropaion is surrounded by other graves, which radiate toward it. Thus it seems that the remains of St. Peter, which would have been among the most jealously guarded relics of the ancient Roman Christian community, had been buried, perhaps immediately after his death, perhaps a brief time later, in the Vatican Hill necropolis: secretly, but with sufficient clues to indicate to pious Christian pilgrims the location of Peter's tomb. Perhaps the remains were, during persecutions, moved to a less risky place and then reinterred. Perhaps the Tropaion was part of a Christian complex that, in calmer times, was used for baptisms, ordinations, and funerals. Perhaps, before the Tropaion was built, the grave itself was used as a site for small Christian gatherings in the dead of night.

No one knows for sure. Archaeology isn't algebra; it yields probabilities rather than certainties. But reputable scientific opinion today holds that the excavations under St. Peter's in the 1940s—originally undertaken for an entirely different purpose—did yield the mortal remains of Peter.

Oddly enough, amid the fragments of Peter's skull, vertebrae, arms, hands, pelvis, and legs, there is nothing from the ankles on down. But perhaps that isn't so odd after all. If a man has been crucified upside down, as tradition says Peter was, the easiest way to remove what was left of his body (which may well have been turned into a living torch during his execution, in another refinement of Roman cruelty) would have been to chop off the deceased's feet and remove the rest of the corpse from its cross.

The remarkable sites beneath St. Peter's are known today as the *scavi* (excavations). A walk through them is a walk into some important truths about what it means to be a Catholic.

---

Not so long ago, you couldn't see St. Peter's from the Tiber River, a few hundred yards away: it was fronted by a Roman slum, the Borgo. To prepare for the holy year of 1950, the Italian government knocked the slums down and built a broad avenue that runs from the Tiber up to St. Peter's Square: the Via della Conciliazione (Reconciliation Street), so named for the 1929 modus vivendi between the Italian Republic and the Church that created the independent microstate of Vatican City. No matter how many times you do it, the turn into the Conciliazione and that first, startling view of St. Peter's and its dome is always breathtaking. We're fortunate to be doing this today because the basilica, whose facade was extensively cleaned for the Great Jubilee of 2000, looks better than it has in centuries, and perhaps ever. What was once a blinding mass of white travertine stone has, on cleaning, revealed itself to be a rich mix of colors, including café au lait and some light pastels. Still, we don't want to concentrate on the facade and the dome as we walk into the square, but on the obelisk that stands precisely in the center of the square, framed by Bernini's great colonnade.

The obelisk, a granite Egyptian monolith standing eighty-four feet tall and weighing 350 tons, was brought to Rome from North Africa by the mad emperor Caligula, who terrorized Rome from A.D. 37 to 41, before he was assassinated by the Praetorian Guard; his wickedness, you may remember, was memorably portrayed by John Hurt in the BBC television series *I, Claudius*. Caligula's nephew, Nero, made the obelisk part of the *spina*, or "spine," of his "circus," an elongated oval in which races were held, mock battles staged, exotic animals exhibited—and the condemned executed, often with unimaginable viciousness, for the amusement of the spectators. As you look to the left of St. Peter's, you can see, past the Swiss Guard standing at the Archway of the Bells, the area of Vatican City known as the Piazza dei Protomartiri Romani (Square of the First Roman Martyrs), so named because that was the part of Nero's now nonexistent circus in which many faithful Christians paid the ultimate price of fidelity.

Tradition tells us that Peter died during one of Nero's spasms of persecution, and if so, he likely died in Nero's circus. If he did, then it's quite possible that the last thing Peter saw on this earth was the obelisk you're now pondering, which was moved to the square in 1586 by Pope Sixtus V. Think about that as we walk a bit farther into the Vatican.

As we enter through the Archway of the Bells, we come to the *scavi* office, the entrance to the excavations beneath the basilica. *Scavi* tours are not large affairs, and as we go down the stairways and enter the excavations themselves, you can see why. The passageways are narrow and slightly musty, even dampish. As we make our way through the dark corridors that were once streets and alleys in the Vatican Hill necropolis, our guide points out the elaborate pagan funerary monuments as well as Christian tombs. There, after about a twenty-minute walk, is what can be made out of the Tropaion. And after that, reinterred in the graffiti-marked wall I mentioned before, are what the guide tells us are the mortal remains of Peter the apostle. Leaving through the gilded baroque splendor of the Clementine Chapel, you can't help but think that what we've just seen and touched and smelled is about as close to the apostolic roots of the Catholic Church as it's possible to get.

The *scavi* are more than excavations; if we take them seriously, the *scavi* demand that we think through the meaning of an extraordinary story involving some utterly ordinary people. Here it is. Sometime in the third decade of the first century of the first millennium of our era, a man named Simon, whose father was named John, made his modest living as a fisherman in Galilee—which, even by regional standards, was a pretty rough patch of what was itself a fringe of the "civilized world." This man, Simon, became a personal friend of Jesus of Nazareth. Through that encounter, he became not Simon but Peter, the rock. But not for a while yet.

His friend Jesus called him "Peter," a wordplay on "rock," but the newly minted Peter hardly seems granitelike in the pre-Easter sections of the Gospels. He is impetuous; he often doesn't understand what Jesus is saying. No sooner does he get his new name than he starts telling Jesus that he, Jesus, is flat wrong when he says that the promised Messiah of God must suffer; Jesus calls him a "Satan" and tells him to "get behind me" (Matthew 16:13–23). When Jesus is arrested, Peter insinuates himself into the courtyard near where his master is being interrogated. But when challenged to acknowledge that he, too, was with Jesus the Galilean,

Peter starts cursing and denies that he ever knew the man. The Gospels do not suggest that Peter was present at the crucifixion; they do tell us that, after his denial, he "went out and wept bitterly" (Matthew 26:69–75).

In the Catholic view of things, Easter changes everything; it certainly changed Peter. After encountering the Risen Christ on Easter Sunday morning and along the lakeshore of the Sea of Galilee, Peter truly *is* the rock. Filled with the Holy Spirit on Pentecost, fifty days after Easter, he becomes the Church's first great evangelist; the tale is told in Acts 2:14–41, where the crowd initially assumes that this suddenly eloquent Galilean fisherman must be drunk—and then converts in great numbers, each hearing Peter in his own language. Peter welcomes the centurion Cornelius, a Gentile, into the Christian fellowship, enabling his fellow Jews to see that God intends the saving message of Christ for the whole world (Acts 10:1–11:18). As the early Church struggles with what it means to be a Christian, Peter is recognized as the center of the Church's unity, the man before whom issues of Christian identity and practice are thrashed out (Acts 15:6–11). Later, according to the most ancient traditions, Peter goes to Rome, where he meets his death—thus fulfilling what the Risen Christ said to him at breakfast along the Sea of Galilee after the miraculous catch of fish: "when you are old, you will stretch out your hands and another will gird you and carry you where you do not wish to go" (John 21:18).

The *scavi* and the obelisk—Peter's remains and the last thing Peter may have seen in this life—confront us with the historical tangibility, the sheer grittiness, of Catholicism. For all that critical scholarship has taught us about the complex story of the early Christian movement, certain unavoidable facts remain. Here, in the *scavi*, you can touch them. A Galilean fisherman—a man whose personal characteristics, warts and all, were carefully recorded by his followers—ends up buried on Vatican Hill. Why? For more than nineteen hundred years, pilgrims from all over the world have come to venerate this man's remains. Why?

Catholicism does not rest on a pious myth, a story that floats away from us the more we try to touch it. Here, in the *scavi*, we're *in touch* with the apostolic foundations of the Catholic Church. And those foundations are not in our minds. They exist, quite literally, in reality. Real things happened to real people who made real, life-and-death decisions—and staked their lives—not on stories or fables but on what they had come to *know* as the truth. Beneath the layers of encrusted tradition and pious storytelling, there is something real, something you can touch, at the bottom of the bottom line of Catholic faith.

And that forces us to confront some decisions.

---

You've asked me to help you explore some of the truths of Catholic faith and practice. One of the most important truths that you might ponder is this: *the truth of faith is something that seizes us*, not something of our own discovery (still less, our invention). The Peter who was led from Galilee to Rome did not make the journey because of something he had discovered and wanted to explore to satisfy his curiosity. Peter went from the security of his modest Galilean fishing business to the dangerous (and ultimately lethal) center of the Roman Empire because he had been seized by the truth, the truth he had met in the person of Jesus.

Being seized by the truth is not cost-free. "You have received without pay, give without pay," Jesus tells his new disciples, including Peter (Matthew 10:8). In Peter's case, the call to give away the truth that had seized and transformed his life eventually cost him his life. And that, too, is a truth to be pondered: *faith in Jesus Christ costs not just something, but everything*. It demands all of us, not just a part of us.

One of the most touching scenes in the Gospels is St. John's story of Peter's encounter with the Risen Christ along the Sea of Galilee, to which I've referred earlier. In that story, the Risen Christ asks Peter, who's surrounded by the other apostles, "Simon, son of John, do you love me more than these?" Peter, perhaps abashed, answers, "Yes, Lord, you know that I love you." The question then comes again, "Do you love me?" And Peter replies, again, "Yes, Lord, you know that I love you." Still evidently unsatisfied, the Risen One poses the question a third time: "Simon, son of John, do you love me?" Peter, the Gospel tells us, was "grieved" because the questions kept coming, and finally answers, "Lord, you know everything, you know that I love you" (John 21:15–17). Generations of preachers have presented this as a matter of the Risen Christ teasing Peter, matching Peter's three denials before the crucifixion with three questions about Peter's love. I think there's something far deeper, something at that border between the intimate and the awesome, going on here.

Peter, who has been given his new name because he is to be the rock on which the Church rests, is being told, gently but firmly, that his love for Christ is not going to be an easy thing. His love is not going to be a matter of "fulfilling" himself. His love must be a pouring out of himself, and in that self-emptying he will find his fulfillment—if not in terms that the world usually understands as "fulfillment." In abandoning any sense of his autonomy, in binding himself to feed the lambs and sheep of the Lord's flock, Peter will find his true freedom. In giving himself away, he will find himself. Freely you have received, freely you must give—if the gift is to continue to live in you. That is what the Risen Christ tells Peter on the lakeshore.

As we've seen, in the Gospels Peter constantly makes a hash of things—which should predispose us to think that those stories really happened; the leader's mistakes and failures and betrayals are not something his followers would likely have invented. In a world deeply skeptical of the miraculous, perhaps the hardest of these stories to accept is the story of Peter's walking on water. Put aside your skepticism for a moment and consider what the story is teaching us—about Peter and about ourselves.

You know the basic narrative. The disciples are out on the Sea of Galilee in a boat by themselves when they see what they take to be a ghost walking toward them across the stormy waters. Jesus tells them not to be afraid: "Take heart, it is I." And Peter, whose crusty skepticism has a modern ring to it, responds, "Lord, if it is you, bid me come to you on the water." Jesus raises the ante: "Come." Peter climbs out of the boat and starts to walk toward Jesus across the water—until, that is, he starts looking around at the waves blown up by the wind, at which point he starts sinking and calls out to Jesus to save him. Jesus takes him by the hand and leads him to safety in the boat, as the weather calms (Matthew 14:25–32).

Did it happen just like that? I don't know, although I'm inclined to think that something extraordinary happened on the Sea of Galilee that night. However we work out the meteorology and hydrology, though, the lesson of the story—the truth it's trying to convey—remains, and helps fill in our portrait of Peter and our understanding of faith as radical gift. When Peter keeps his eyes fixed on Jesus, he can do what he imagines impossible: "walk on water." When he starts looking around for his security—when he starts looking elsewhere—he sinks. So do we. When we keep our gaze fixed on Christ, we, too, can do what seems impossible. We can accept the gift of faith, with humility and gratitude. We can live our lives as the gift for others that our lives are to us. We can discover the depths of ourselves in the emptying of ourselves.

In the Catholic view of things, "walking on water" is an entirely sensible thing to do. It's staying in the boat, hanging tightly to our own sad little securities, that's rather mad.

---

There are many other Peter stories we could revisit—including, while we're here in Rome, the famous *Quo Vadis* story of Peter's alleged flight from Nero's persecution. As the legend has it, Peter decided to flee Rome at the outbreak of persecution, perhaps in fear, perhaps because he thought "the rock" should be somewhere safe so others could eventually find and cling to it, and to him. Heading out the Via Appia, Peter meets Jesus, who's heading *into* the city and the persecution. "Quo vadis, Domine," Peter asks—"Lord, where are you going?" "I am going to Rome to be crucified," Jesus answers—and disappears. At which point Peter turns back into the city to embrace martyrdom. In Rome, to this day, you can visit the spot on the Via Appia Antica where all of this is said to have happened (the church is worth a visit; the Quo Vadis Restaurant is a tourist trap).

The *Quo Vadis* legend is interesting for its tenacity. It's also interesting for the same reason it's interesting that the Church, in deciding which books to include in the canon of the New Testament, included four Gospels that all describe, sometimes in great detail, Peter's failures. Those stories could have been discretely edited out, airbrushed from history; they weren't. And that tells us something.

What it tells us is that weakness and failure have been part of the Catholic reality *from the beginning*. Weakness and failure, too, are part of the grittiness of Catholicism—including weakness and failure, stupidity and cowardice among the Church's ordained leaders. Flannery O'Connor was speaking a very ancient truth when she wrote in 1955 that "it seems to be a fact that you have to suffer as much from the Church as for it." Almost fifty years later, Catholics in the United States have relearned that lesson the hard way, in the scandal of clerical sexual abuse and the crisis that scandal caused when it was so badly handled by some bishops—the successors of the apostles. I don't detect any massive abandonment of the Catholic Church because of this crisis. But it does force us to come to grips with the fact that the people of the Church, including its ordained leadership, are earthen vessels carrying the treasure of faith in history (as St. Paul put it in 2 Corinthians 4:7).

Only the naive would expect it to be otherwise. Like Peter, all the people of the Church, including the Church's ordained leadership, must constantly be purified. And purified by what? Like Peter, we must be purified by love, by a more complete and radical emptying of self. "Smugness," Flannery O'Connor once wrote, "is the Great Catholic Sin." Looking at Peter, we might almost say, "as it was in the beginning . . ."

But here, too, the *scavi* help us get to the deeper truth of Catholic things. Although the early Church insisted on including weakness and failure in the narrative of its first years and decades, the story line of the New Testament—of the Gospels and the Acts of the Apostles—is not, finally, a story of failure, but of purified love transforming the world. To be sure, that transformation comes with a price: imagine Peter, in the agonized moments before his death, looking at that obelisk we can see today, and you can understand that none of this is easy. Then consider all those pilgrims who, like Peter, were seized by the truth of Christ and who have come, over the centuries, to place themselves in the presence of Peter's remains. Pious nostalgia? Raw curiosity? I don't think so. Whether articulate or mute, what those millions of other lives are saying, as they pray in the *scavi* or over the *scavi*, surrounded by the baroque magnificence of the basilica, is that *failure is not the final word.* Emptiness and oblivion are not our destiny. Love is the final word. And love is the most living thing of all because love is of God.

To know that, and to stake your life on it, is to have been seized by the truth of God in Christ—amid and through, not around, the gritty reality of the world.

3

## St. Catherine's Monastery, Mount Sinai/The Holy Sepulcher, Jerusalem—The Face of Christ

As you saw in Milledgeville, Georgia, the "Catholic world" isn't confined to sites owned or operated by the Catholic Church. In this letter, I'd like to take you to two different kinds of sites within the "Catholic world": one is a Greek Orthodox monastery; the second is a church divided among a gaggle of Christian communities who can (and do) argue for decades about which of them gets to fix the roof. As I've said before, Catholicism and grittiness go together. Let's go now to two very gritty places located on the border of the divine and the human—places where *things happened*, things with ultimate consequences.

---

No one knows for certain where Mount Sinai, the mountain where God met Moses in the Hebrew Bible, is located. A pilgrimage tradition that dates back to about

A.D. 400 identifies "Mount Sinai" with Jebel Mûsā, a 7,500-foot twin-peaked mountain at the southern tip of the Sinai Peninsula. The landscape seems appropriate to the story. Jebel Mûsā is a steep, craggy place, with two neighboring mountains close at hand and a large plain at the base of the mountain cluster; its colors and topography are reminiscent of the stark beauty of the American Southwest. Arguments about the precise location of biblical sites have fueled doctoral dissertations beyond numbering; most expert opinion today agrees that the early Christian pilgrims got it right—Jebel Mûsā (Mountain of Moses) is the site of the encounter at the burning bush, the giving of the Ten Commandments, and the Mosaic covenant made between God and the people of Israel.

After twelve centuries of Islamic dominance, it's easy to forget that the Egyptian desert was the cradle of monasticism in early Christian history, beginning with St. Anthony in the mid-third century. These monks led lives of extraordinary, even desperate rigor, none more so than the "anchorites" or "eremites" who lived by themselves in small hermitages. Once the word got around, through pilgrims, that Jebel Mûsā was where some of the most dramatic events in the book of Exodus had unfolded, hermitages sprang up on the shadier northern slope of the mountain, the traditional site of the burning bush through which Moses first encountered the God of Abraham, Isaac, and Jacob. In 527, the Byzantine emperor Justinian built a great monastery on that same northern slope. High, thick walls had to be erected later to protect the monks from robbers; a modus vivendi was achieved still later with invading Muslims by allowing them to build a small mosque inside the compound. If you talk to the Bedouins who have provided security at St. Catherine's for a very long time, they'll tell you that this is where they come to venerate Moses, whom they regard as a prophet.

Justinian dedicated the monastery church to Mary and to the commemoration of Christ's transfiguration; in the eighth century, when the relics of St. Catherine of Alexandria were brought to Jebel Mûsā for safekeeping, the whole complex was renamed in her honor. Today the Monastery of St. Catherine is an autonomous Orthodox church, and its abbot (or hegumen, in Orthodox terminology) is consecrated by the Greek Orthodox patriarch of Jerusalem with the impressive title "Archbishop of Sinai, Pharan, and Raitho." For all its isolation, and notwithstanding the harshness of the surrounding area, St. Catherine's is a living Christian community, its two dozen monks offering pastoral care to some nine thousand local Christians, most of them Red Sea fishermen.

The same monks also care for some of the greatest treasures in the Christian world: the Codex Sinaiticus, one of the earliest extant copies of the Greek Bible, discovered by the German biblical scholar Constantin Tischendorf in the monastery library in 1844; the Codex Syriacus, a fourth-century rendering of the Gospels in Syriac; some three thousand other manuscripts in Arabic, Georgian, and Slavonic as well as Syriac and Greek; and an incomparable collection of icons.

One of those icons is why we've come to this place, where timelessness is tangible. It's the perfect setting in which to ponder the truths embodied by St. Catherine's most famous icon, Christos Pantokrator—Christ the All-Sovereign, Christ the Universal King.

A word about icons and the first-millennium controversy over "iconoclasm" is in order. First, icons.

An icon is not intended to be a work of representational art, in the usual way that we think of paintings by, say, Rembrandt. Rather, an icon is "written" (not "painted") by an iconographer, for whom his work is both a vocation (not merely a job) and a form of prayer: an iconographer "writes" icons because he believes himself called by God to do so, and he writes specific icons as the result of meditation and prayer on some mystery of the faith. The product, the icon, is intended to be another border place between the divine and the human, a window into the mystery that it pictorially conveys.

In terms of Western theological terminology, and with apologies to the learned for the anachronism, an icon is a *symbol* that *makes present* what it conveys. A conventional Western painting—Holbein's portrait of Sir Thomas More—simply says, "This is what this man looked like." Holbein didn't intend to make Sir Thomas *present*, in the sense that those viewing the painting would "meet" the former lord chancellor and "man for all seasons." The anonymous iconographic genius who wrote Christos Pantokrator intended precisely that: in the Christos Pantokrator we meet Jesus Christ, the Lord.

How can this be? To go back to Moses and the Ten Commandments: what happened to the Bible's condemnation of idolatry, its absolute prohibition against pictorial or other artistic representations of God? How is an icon not an idol?

When the Christian movement largely displaced the gods of Greek and Roman antiquity, everyone, whether Christian or not, might well have imagined that this meant the death of religious art. Mainstream Christianity accepted the Hebrew Bible as divine revelation, and that meant (in the wonderful translation done by King James's committee) "Thou shalt not make unto thee any graven image" (Exodus 20:4). When Christianity met the neo-Platonic thought that dominated the Mediterranean world, some Christian philosophers began to teach that the "image of God" in us, and preeminently in Christ, is located in the "rational soul"—and you can't paint or sculpt or make a mosaic representation of the rational soul. For these thinkers, attempts to portray the "image of God" in us was both idolatrous and philosophically absurd. Had they won the day, religious art would have been doomed.

Yet the triumph of Christianity in the Roman world actually produced an extraordinary and unprecedented outpouring of artistic creativity that continues to this day. What happened? The grittiest, most earthy of Christian claims—that the Son of God became flesh in Jesus of Nazareth—eventually became the rationale for both Christian iconography and Christian representational art. Rather than negate art, the Incarnation became the ultimate warrant for religious art. This is worth thinking about for a moment.

The theological battle between the iconoclasts, who literally destroyed icons, and the defenders of icons lasted for almost two hundred years. A lot of blood was spilled as the Byzantine emperors got into the fray, and what must have been some of the greatest religious art in history was destroyed in the process. Although the politics of the controversy dragged on until 843, the issue was resolved theologically in 787 at the Second Council of Nicaea. The argument that prevailed was an argument from grittiness: it turned on the tangibility, so to speak, of Christ, the incarnate Son of God.

At Nicaea II the icon defenders told their iconoclastic adversaries, yes, of course we agree that the Son is the Image of God the Father; that's what the Council of Chalcedon declared in 451 and we all accept that. But you iconoclasts are missing the further point: the Image of the Father has been made human in the incarnation. When Mary said yes to the angel Gabriel's startling message, *the Image of God became a man*. Jesus Christ was not a crypto-human, God in a fleshly disguise; and to take that seriously means taking the physical and the material seriously. That brings us to icons.

As the Yale historian Jaroslav Pelikan puts it, summarizing the winning argument in this debate, an icon is "not an idol but an image of the Image." Indeed, Pelikan reports, the defenders of icons pushed their argument all the way back, proposing that the "making of images" begins within God himself: for the Son is the Image of the Father and through this Image—this Second Person of the Trinity, this Logos, this Word—God creates the world. Everything in the world is part of what Pelikan calls a "great chain of images," whose origins are within the interior life of God the Holy Trinity.

What about idolatry?

Idolatry, the defenders of icons taught, was the arrogant human attempt to "get at" and control the divine through images, to cross the infinite gulf between the human and the divine by our own efforts. What happened in the Incarnation, they continued, is that *that gulf was crossed for us*. Jesus Christ, truly divine and truly human, is the living, enfleshed Image that completes the great chain of images—the incarnate Son of God who brings the divine into the human world and lifts the human up into the interior life of God himself. God, who once forbade the people of Israel to make images of himself, has given us the true Image, and in the flesh. When God enters history, the events of salvation history, "written" iconographically for us, can become true images of the Image.

Whew.

I'd apologize for this brief and admittedly high-altitude theological detour, except that it's very important in nailing down a theme we've already touched on: *Catholicism is realism*. Why was the iconoclastic controversy so important? The defenders of icons were right, and the Church was right to vindicate them, because what was at stake here was nothing less than the Christian claim that *we can touch the truth of our salvation*. Christianity, even in its most abstract neo-Platonic dress, is not simply a matter of ideas, even true ideas. Christianity is a matter of truths enfleshed: God become man, and man deified.

---

That is the One we meet in the Christos Pantokrator.

Because it lies so far from the beaten track, St. Catherine's and its icons escaped the ravages of the iconoclasts. Discovered under layers of paint, the Christos Pantokrator is an image of Christ in a typical iconographic pose, full-face toward us, the Lord's head surrounded by a golden corona or halo, his left arm clutching a jeweled Bible to himself (the Word of God, the Second Person of the Trinity, holding the Word of God, the Holy Scripture), his right hand raised in a gesture that is both greeting and blessing, the thumb and ring finger touching (in acknowledgment of the two natures united in the one person of Christ), the index and middle fingers crossed (in acknowledgment of the instrument of salvation). The colors are impressively rich: gold and ivory, lavender and vermilion. But it is the Holy Face—majestic, calm, strikingly masculine—that draws us into the icon and into an encounter with the Lord himself.

It is one face, for Christ is one. Yet the iconographer, by writing a face with two subtly different expressions, has drawn us into the mystery of God incarnate, the Son of God come in the flesh. For all its humanity, we see—perhaps better, we *sense*—that, while this is a truly human face, it's unlike any face we've seen before. He is in time, in one dimension of his face, but beyond time, in another. He is like every other human person, (i.e., a person of time and space and history), but he is also transcendent, eternal. We meet him in his humanity; he draws us into his divinity. As Professor Pelikan writes, he is the embodiment of three transcendentals: the "one who was the embodiment not only of the True in his teaching and of the Good in his life, but of the Beautiful in his form as 'the fairest of the sons of men' (Psalm 45.2)." In the truth, goodness, and beauty of his majesty, we glimpse the glory of our own human destiny, if we believe in him and his power to transform our lives into a share in his own divine life. The true, the good, and the beautiful meet in Christ, the Image of the Father from all eternity, the son of Mary of Nazareth according to the flesh.

The Christos Pantokrator, which was probably written in Constantinople in the sixth century, iconographically embodies a theme that was key to the teaching of the Second Vatican Council in the twentieth century: in Jesus Christ we meet both the truth of the merciful Father and the truth about our humanity. As the Council fathers wrote, "Christ, the final Adam, by the revelation of the mystery of the Father and His love, fully reveals man to man himself and makes his supreme calling clear" (*Gaudium et Spes*, 22).

"Spirituality," as defined in those hundreds of books you find shelved under that topic in any megastore, is our search for the "religious." Catholicism is emphatically *not* "spirituality" in that sense of the term. Catholicism (according to the great twentieth-century Swiss theologian Hans Urs von Balthasar) is about God's search for us—and our "search" involves our learning, over the course of a lifetime, to take the same path through history that God does. Human reason, the Catholic Church insists, can "get" us to God, in the sense that human reason can "find" the fact of God's existence through rational argument. But we cannot meet the God of Abraham, Isaac, and Jacob, the God who is the Father of Jesus Christ, by reason alone, nor can we discover God's attributes. That required a demonstration—and the demonstration of the truth about God, the merciful Father, comes through the Incarnation of the Son of God, who shows us the Father and his mercy.

You've heard since you were a child about the parable of the "prodigal son" (Luke 15:11–32), which is more accurately called the parable of the merciful father. Yes, the profligate son sets the dramatic stage by his dissipation and his (rather calculating) decision to return home as a hired hand. But it's the father, who watches from afar and runs out to greet his wayward son before he arrives, who is the center of the dramatic action. It's the father who casts all pragmatism, all rational calculation, aside—who cannot imagine taking his son back as a hireling but lavishly embraces him and welcomes him home as a son. The merciful Father revealed by Jesus Christ does not wait for us to figure out our dependency, nor does he respond to our acknowledgment of our failures by bringing us "home" in a lesser station. He, too, comes in search of us: he rushes out to embrace us, to restore to us what is ours by heritage—that which we have lost by our own squalid selfishness. In his incarnate Son, the merciful Father wishes to make us sons and daughters again. In language that the writer of the Christos Pantokrator might have used, what he offers us, profligately and freely, is *theosis*, "divinization," the restoration of what he intended for us in the beginning, but which we lost by our willfulness.

This is the "good news" of the gospel—but there is more. As the Second Vatican Council insisted, and as we learn as we're drawn into the Christos Pantokrator, *Jesus Christ reveals who we are*, as well as *who God is*. And who we think we are has a lot to do with the unfolding of modern history. Let me show you how.

---

In June 1959 the commission preparing the agenda for the Second Vatican Council wrote to all the bishops of the world, asking them what they'd like to talk about. The answers, from all over the world, fill the first several volumes of the *Acta*, the official record of Vatican II. Some of the proposals strikingly anticipate the key themes that would dominate the council's debates: the shape of Catholic worship, the relationship of Scripture and Tradition in God's revelation, the role of the local bishop and the "college" of bishops, religious freedom as a human right. But what's even more striking, to someone who thumbs through the first volumes of the *Acta*, is how mundane many of the submissions are. Clearly many bishops did not expect the council to undertake a root-and-branch examination of Catholic self-understanding and practice. Anticipating a brief, clear-cut council in which their role would be to ratify documents pre-prepared in Rome, many bishops were far more concerned to have addressed the mundane matters they worried about on a daily basis: some wanted various modest changes in canon law; others wanted to be able to give permissions or grant exemptions from this or that without referring the matter to Rome. If you read the *Acta*'s opening volumes, you get the distinct impression that many bishops imagined that Vatican II would be an exercise in ecclesiastical housekeeping. (My favorite submission came from the archbishop of Washington, D.C., Patrick J. O'Boyle. After listing a half dozen or so housekeeping items, Archbishop O'Boyle proposed that the council pronounce, "in light of the doctrines of creation and redemption," on "the possibility of intelligent life on other planets." When I read that in a Roman archive, I laughed out loud—it's even funnier in Latin—and the archivist asked me what was so funny. To which I could only reply, "Well, after fifteen years of working there, I should have thought that the first thing the archbishop of Washington would have wanted to determine was the possibility of intelligent life in his own diocese.")

Amid all that paper in the *Acta* you can find the submission from the forty-year-old auxiliary bishop of Kraków, a philosophically inclined Pole named Karol Wojtyła, whom very few people in Rome had ever heard of. Wojtyła didn't send a laundry list of ecclesiastical housekeeping chores. He sent a kind of philosophical essay, built around a single, sharp question—what in the world *happened*? How did a twentieth century that had begun with such high expectations for the human future produce, within five decades, two world wars, three totalitarian systems, Auschwitz, the Gulag, mountains of corpses, oceans of blood, the greatest persecutions in Christian history, and a cold war that threatened the future of the planet? *What happened*?

What happened, Karol Wojtyła suggested, was that the great project of Western humanism had gone off the rails. Desperately defective ideas of the human person, married to modern technology, had turned the twentieth century into a slaughterhouse. Ideas have consequences, and bad ideas can have lethal consequences. In the first half of the twentieth century, perhaps as many as a hundred million human beings paid with their lives for the consequences of some desperately defective ideas of *who we are*.

What was to be done? Wojtyła proposed that the Catholic Church undertake a gigantic intellectual, cultural, and spiritual rescue mission. The Church should help rescue humanism—rescue the whole project of modernity—by proposing once again, with full clarity and conviction, that we see the true meaning of our humanity in the face of Christ. In Christ, we meet the truth that man without God has lost touch with the deepest yearnings of his humanity. In Christ, we meet the truth that willfulness is not freedom but a form of slavery. In Christ we meet the truth that men and women who live their lives against a horizon of transcendent possibility are the true servants of human betterment here and now. In Christ, we meet the Father, whose mercy redeems our humanity and fulfills its true destiny, which is an eternal destiny. Humanism without God is unhuman, and ultimately inhuman. As St. Augustine wrote in his *Confessions*, "Thou hast made us for Thyself, O Lord, and our hearts are restless until they rest in Thee." The restless yearnings of the modern heart will be satisfied in Christ; a Christ-centered humanism is a true and ennobling humanism.

---

As I said a moment ago, the truth about God and about us that the Catholic Church carries in history required a demonstration. That demonstration was the life of Jesus Christ, culminating in the events of Christ's passion, death, and resurrection. So let's go now to the site where tradition tells us the drama of salvation reached its final act.

Entering the Old City of Jerusalem through the Jaffa Gate, we walk about a hundred yards until we turn left into David Street, full of Arab suqs. The shallow steps of David Street take us another sixty yards or so until we reach Christian Quarter Road, into which we make another left turn; the vast stone blocks in the pavement date from the time of Herod the Great. A sign directs us into a covered street on the right; by following it to its end, we turn left into the courtyard in front of the Church of the Holy Sepulcher.

You'll find it disorienting, for it hardly seems, on walking in, like a single "church" at all, but rather a jumble of shrines. Stepping inside the front door, we're immediately confronted with a stone embedded in the floor. Tradition calls it the "Stone of Unction," where the body of Jesus was anointed after it was taken down from the cross; it is jointly "owned" by the Armenian Apostolic Church, the Greek Orthodox Church, and the Catholic Church. To our right, up nineteen steep, winding stone steps, is a kind of loft containing two major shrines, one cared for by the Catholic Church and one by the Orthodox Church: this is the traditional site of

Calvary and the eleventh and twelfth stations of the cross—Jesus being nailed to the cross and Jesus crucified. Between the two chapels in the loft is the thirteenth station, the Stabat Mater, where a Catholic altar commemorates Mary receiving the dead body of her son in the famous pose known the world over from Michelangelo's *Pietà*.

If we turn left at the Stone of Unction, we wind our way around to an enormous square stone structure supported by ugly steel girders, erected to counter the damage caused by an earthquake in 1927. This is the Aedicule. The area surrounding it, the Anastasis (Resurrection), is surmounted by a rotunda, recently restored and decorated in a slightly delirious, modern Italian style; it took decades for the squabbling Orthodox, Armenians, and Catholics to agree on its restoration, despite the ever-present possibility of its collapse. Inside the Aedicule are two chapels, the first called the Chapel of the Angel, who met the surprised women on Easter morning (Matthew 28:2–7; Mark 16:5–7). A low doorway gives access to the second chapel; marble-lined and filled with candles, it is so small that only three people can kneel inside at once. Here, according to tradition, lay the body of Jesus from late Good Friday afternoon until Easter. An officious Orthodox monk hustles pilgrims and tourists in and out, his hand held out for an "offering." Against the back wall on the outside of the Aedicule, a Coptic monk conducts prayers and services in a loud voice, some of which strikes the untrained ear as a barely disguised protest at the Copts' exclusion from responsibility for the Aedicule. But the Copts have less to complain of than the Ethiopian Orthodox, who are confined to a ramshackle "monastery" on the roof, the monks' cells being corrugated steel sheds that remind you of the sweat box from which Alec Guinness conducted his battle of wits with Colonel Saito in *The Bridge on the River Kwai*. If you come to the 6:30 A.M. Sunday Mass conducted by the Franciscans at the Aedicule, you will notice that, at the precise stroke of 7:30 A.M., the "Catholic rug" is rolled up from the front of the Aedicule and the "Orthodox rug" put back down.

At first blush, it's hard not to think of all this as a shambles—and a disgraceful shambles at that. The noise, the smells, the poor lighting, the rather garish rotunda dome, the barely repressed competition of the various Christian communities (whose relations are governed, to this day, by a status quo imposed by the Ottoman Turks, as the quarreling factions can agree on nothing else)—all of this seems not simply strange but scandalous. Christians conducting a form of civil war over what they all agree are the most important places in human history?

And yet, and yet . . . you notice, it being a Sunday morning, that the Mass being celebrated by the Franciscans is not the usual Mass for that Sunday, but the Mass of Easter—and you join in the simple Latin antiphon, *Haec dies quam fecit Dominus, exultemus et laetemur in ea* (This is the day the Lord has made, let us rejoice and be glad in it), reminded, as you've never been before, that every Sunday *is* Easter, the day of the Lord's resurrection. After Mass, you notice the pilgrim, lost in silent prayer at the back of the twelfth station, the tears running through the hands covering his face. Then you kiss the rock of Calvary, and the Stone of Unction, and the Holy Sepulcher itself—and none of the rest makes any difference at all. Then the squawking Copts and the emaciated Ethiopians and the surly Greek Orthodox and the torpid Franciscans all seem somehow transformed. If

God came searching for us in history, if the Son of God redeemed us in the flesh, then why be repelled by the grittiness of it all? God wasn't, and neither was God's Son.

And then you understand that the Greek Orthodox are right to have named a spot on the marble floor of their cathedral, opposite the Aedicule, the *omphalos* (navel). This *is* the center of the world, the center of history.

---

One writer who understood that was the great English novelist and Catholic convert, Evelyn Waugh. You may have a hard time finding a copy of what most critics have declared to be one of Waugh's decidedly minor efforts, *Helena*, but it's well worth searching out and reading. Waugh himself thought it his "most ambitious work," and beneath its veneer of technical experimentation—as a young woman, the Empress Helena, mother of Constantine (who built the first Basilica of the Holy Sepulcher in 325), talks like a British teenager of the flapper era—the novelist was constructing a fictional account of the confrontation between myth and history. *Something had happened*, Helena was convinced, and she was determined to find what Waugh described in a letter as "the essential physical historical fact of the redemption"—the True Cross of Christ.

In this deceptively simple novel, Waugh took on the false humanisms of which young Bishop Karol Wojtyła wrote in his letter to the commission preparing the agenda of Vatican II. To Waugh, what admirable but muddle-headed naturalistic humanists like Aldous Huxley (*Brave New World*) and George Orwell (*1984*) didn't understand was that modern agnostic or atheistic humanism was a variant on Christianity's ancient foe, gnosticism: the heresy that denies the importance, even the reality, of the material world. At bottom, gnosticism is a denial of the essential facts of life, including the facts of suffering and death. The True Cross, for which Helena searches in her old age, is the emblem of both our createdness and our redeemedness—this "remorseless lump of wood, to which Christ was nailed in agony," as one Waugh biographer puts it. That is what we confront in the Church of the Holy Sepulcher. Without that grittiness, Christianity is just another of the mystery cults of the ancient Mediterranean world. With this "remorseless lump of wood," a tangible witness to the mystery of the Incarnation, the window to the supernatural is open, and the "real world" in both its agonies and its joys is put into proper perspective—the perspective of the Kingdom of God, which breaks into the world and history through the life, death, and resurrection of Jesus Christ.

Evelyn Waugh had all this in mind when he wrote Orwell, thanking him for a gift copy of *1984*, Orwell's great dystopian novel of the terrors of a totalitarian future. Waugh complimented Orwell on his novelistic ingenuity. But then he wrote that "the book failed to make my flesh creep as presumably you intended." Why? Because "men who have loved a crucified God need never think of torture as all-powerful."

Indeed, as Catholicism thinks of these things, men and women who have loved a crucified God are the true humanists, because they have been given the grace of knowing, in their flesh, the true measure of our humanity, redeemed at such a cost and destined for glory. That is why, on March 26, 2000, something happened in the Church of the Holy Sepulcher, away from the eyes of the world, that speaks volumes about this place and its meaning. It was Pope John Paul II's last afternoon in Jerusalem, after a week-long pilgrimage to the Holy Land that had riveted international attention. During one of the last formal events of the day, a lunch at the residence of the papal representative, the Pope quietly asked if he might be permitted to go back to the Church of the Holy Sepulcher, where he had celebrated a televised Mass that morning—privately, as an ordinary pilgrim. The authorities agreed, and John Paul, almost eighty years old, a man who walked with difficulty and pain, climbed those nineteen stone steps to the twelfth station of the cross to pray. This old Polish priest, who had displayed unshakable courage in the face of the worst of modern tyrannies, was determined to pray at Calvary, the place where all the world's fears had been offered by the Son to the Father, in order to set humanity free from fear. And he did, meeting a deep longing of his own Christian soul and vindicating the proposal he had urged on the Second Vatican Council forty years before—that the Church should bear witness to the Christ who reveals to us *who we are* and thereby enables us to be truly, fully, radically human.

"And the Word became flesh and dwelt among us, full of grace and truth; we have beheld his glory, glory as of the only Son from the Father" (John 1:14). *He* is the true measure of *who we are*. In his Holy Face, we meet the truth about ourselves, in the flesh.

# 4

# The Dormition Abbey, Jerusalem—Mary and Discipleship

Just south of the Old City of Jerusalem is Mount Zion, the site of King David's original fortress (the "City of David," 2 Samuel 5:7). Mount Zion has been a battle site for millennia. Around 1000 B.C., David captured an ancient Jebusite acropolis called Zion and refortified it as his own city (hence the "City of David"); from this starting point David made adjacent Jerusalem (which had never belonged to the territory of any Israelite tribe) the capital of his unified monarchy. The Crusaders built a church dedicated to Mary here in 1100; it was destroyed by the sultan of Damascus in 1219. About three thousand years after David conquered the Jebusite stronghold, Mount Zion was again a battleground, during Israel's 1948 War of Independence and the 1967 Six Day War. As we come through Zion Gate, you'll notice the bullet holes in the white Jerusalem stone of the Old City walls.

Mount Zion is thick with history and memory. The cenotaph of David is here, as is the traditional site of the

Cenacle, the room in which Jesus celebrated his last supper with his disciples, and the room in which the disciples later received the Holy Spirit on Pentecost. From Mount Zion, we can look south to the pool of Siloam, where Jesus performed a miraculous cure (John 9:7); east over the Kidron Valley to the Monument of Absalom, David's rebellious son; and slightly northeast to the Mount of Olives, where we see the gnarled olive trees of the Garden of Gethsemane and a most touching piece of Jerusalem architecture—the tear-shaped Church of the Dominus Flevit, which reminds us that "the Lord wept" (*Dominus flevit*) over his beloved Jerusalem before his death (Luke 19:41–44).

We've come to Mount Zion to visit the Dormition Abbey, which is about a hundred yards or so south of the Old City walls. Its striking octagonal stone structure, distinctive conical roof, and handsome bell tower make it one of the city's most visible landmarks. It was built by Kaiser Wilhelm II, who had been given a parcel of land on Mount Zion by Sultan Abdul Hamid II during the German emperor's visit to Jerusalem in 1898; the kaiser's architect took as his model the cathedral in Aachen where Charlemagne is buried (which was itself modeled on the great octagonal church of S. Vitale in Ravenna). That bit of imperial place marking notwithstanding, the Dormitio (as the locals call it) is a magnificent building. Just beyond the sometimes jarring bustle of the Old City, it is an oasis of calm and quiet. Its circular interior, surmounted by that conical roof, breathes the spacious openness of transcendence. A splendid golden mosaic of the Virgin and Child focuses our attention in the apse; beneath are mosaic portraits of the prophets who foretold the Messiah's coming: Isaiah and Jeremiah, Ezekiel and Daniel; Haggai, Malachi, Micah, and Zechariah.

The floor beneath the dome is another gem of the mosaicist's art. A series of concentric circles represents the spread of God's saving Word throughout the world, which begins from within the Holy Trinity itself; thus the inner ring contains three interlocking circles, each with the word *hagios* (holy), reminding us of the one God who is three Divine Persons. The adjoining circle depicts the *traditio* (tradition, or "handing on") of the Word announced to the world with the names of the four major prophets (Isaiah, Jeremiah, Ezekiel, Daniel), while the third circle commemorates the twelve minor prophets (Hosea, Joel, Amos, Obadiah, Jonah, Micah, Nahum, Habakkuk, Zephaniah, Haggai, Zechariah, and Malachi). The fourth circle contains the Christian evangelists, depicted by their traditional symbols: a man (Matthew), a lion (Mark), a calf (Luke), and an eagle (John). Then comes the circle of the twelve apostles (in which, interestingly enough, Paul, not Matthias, takes the place of Judas Iscariot). The apostolic circle touches a circle depicting the months of the year and the signs of the zodiac, which Christian artists sometimes use to represent the totality of the universe. The mosaic is completed by a final circle, a Latin rendering of Proverbs 8:23 and its paean to divine Wisdom: "He formed me from of old, from eternity, before the earth. The abyss did not exist when I was born, the springs of the sea had not gushed forth, the mountains were not set in their place, nor the hills when I was born."

As magnificent as the Dormitio is, though, we're not here to admire the architecture and art, or even to spend time in the main body of the church. Rather, we want to go downstairs to the crypt, to think about Mary, the mother of Jesus and the mother of the Church. Through Mary, we can think about the mystery of vocation—of "being called"—which is at the center of the Catholic life.

---

No one knows where Mary lived out her life after the Resurrection or where she died. (One of the more intriguing arguments for the bodily "assumption" of Mary into heaven, which was defined as an article of Catholic faith in 1950, is the quite remarkable fact that there is no site in the Christian world at which the pious have ever seriously claimed to hold the relics of Mary—which would surely have been a place of pilgrimage.) One venerable tradition has Mary dying in Ephesus, where it is assumed that her guardian, the apostle John, was living. Another tradition has Mary living out her life on Mount Zion and "falling asleep" here. Thus the formal name of this great church is the Dormitio Sanctae Mariae, the Church of the Falling Asleep of St. Mary.

The tradition of Mary's "dormition" on Mount Zion is embodied in a small shrine at the center of the crypt. There, atop a cenotaph, is a life-size statue of the Virgin "asleep," carved from ivory and cherry wood. Keeping watch from the interior of a small cupola above are some of the prominent women of the Old Testament, depicted in mosaics: Eve, mother of humanity; Miriam, sister of Moses and songstress of Israel's liberation; Jael, the Kenite who defends Israel from the Canaanite warrior Sisera; Judith, the beautiful widow who saves Jerusalem from the army of Nebuchadnezzar; Ruth, the faithful Moabite who becomes the great-grandmother of King David; and Esther, who saves her exiled Jewish kinsmen from the murderous plot of Haman.

Here, in the quiet of the Dormitio's crypt, is as good a place as I know to ponder the meaning of Mary for Catholics.

Mary is both an invitation to Catholicism and, for many Protestants, an obstacle to Catholicism. Curiously enough, Mary was also a bit of an obstacle at one point in the spiritual journey of a very Catholic young Pole named Karol Wojtyła, who grew up in a land of Marian piety and later became Pope John Paul II. John Paul is the first pope to publish a memoir of his struggle to discern his Christian vocation, *Gift and Mystery*. He tells us that when he left his hometown, Wadowice, to enter the Jagiellonian University in Kraków in 1938, he felt burdened by the traditional Marian piety of his birthplace: "I began to question my devotion to Mary, believing that, if it became too great, it might end up compromising the supremacy of the worship owed to Christ."

During the brutal Nazi occupation of Kraków in World War II, Karol Wojtyła started reading the French theologian St. Louis Grignion de Montfort (1673–1716). Montfort's masterwork, *True Devotion to Mary*, taught Wojtyła that all true Marian piety was Christ-centered—all "true devotion to Mary" *necessarily* pointed us to Christ, and through Christ (who is both son of Mary and Son of God) into the mystery of God himself, God the Holy Trinity. Montfort's language is a bit ornate for contemporary tastes (John Paul gently refers to the Frenchman's "rather florid and baroque style"), but he got the essential point right: rather than an obstacle to an encounter with the living Christ, Mary was and is a privileged vehicle for meeting Christ the Lord.

The New Testament itself supports Montfort's proposal. The last words of Mary recorded in the Gospels—

"Do whatever he tells you," her instruction to the waiters at the wedding feast of Cana (John 2:5)—sum up Mary's singular role in the history of salvation: Mary is the unique witness who, from the moment of the Incarnation, always points beyond herself ("Do whatever *he* tells you") to her son. And because her son in the flesh is also the incarnate Son of God, by pointing us to her son Mary also points us into the heart of the Trinity. All "true devotion to Mary," in Montfort's phrase, is Christocentric and Trinitarian: all true Marian piety is an invitation to a deeper encounter with the mystery of the Incarnation and the mystery of the Trinity. All true Marian piety is thus an invitation to a deeper reflection on *who we are* and *who God is*. It *must* be, to be true to itself.

---

Contemporary Catholic theology has developed this insight in intriguing ways that give a rich texture to the Church's Marian piety. We've already met the Swiss theologian Hans Urs von Balthasar, a kind of pyrotechnic genius of the modern Catholic world. Thinking through the complex reality of the Church in one of his books, *The Office of Peter and the Structure of the Church*, Balthasar suggest that the Church in every age is formed in the image of the great figures of the New Testament. The Church of proclamation and evangelization, for example, is formed in thc image of St. Paul, the great apostle of the Gentiles. The Church of contemplation and mystical insight is constantly being formed in the image of the apostle John, the beloved disciple who rested his head on the Lord's chest at the Last Supper. The Church of authority is formed in the image of Peter, to whom

Christ gave the power of the keys, the power to bind and loose, and the parallel injunction to "strengthen your brethren" (Luke 22:32). And the Church of discipleship—*which is the basis of everything else*—is formed in the image of a woman, Mary, who is the first of disciples and thus the mother of the Church.

How? Because it is in Mary's *fiat*—"Be it done unto me according to *your* word" (Luke 1:38)—that we discover the pattern or form of all Christian discipleship. Mary's fiat makes possible the incarnation of the Son of God, whose redeeming and sanctifying work in history continues in the Church through its proclamation, contemplation, and authority. Mary is the first disciple of the son she bore and nursed and raised; because all Christians are grafted onto Christ in baptism, Mary is the mother of the Church, the mystical body of Christ extended in history. Through Mary's *fiat,* we glimpse one of the primary lessons of discipleship, a lesson it takes a lifetime to learn: *we are not in charge of our lives—God is in charge of our lives.* To know that is to be liberated in the truest sense of human freedom. To know that is to be set free from the restlessness that besets every human heart in every age.

Mary's articulated *fiat* at the Annunciation—"Be it done unto me according to your word"—is completed by Mary's silent *fiat,* the reception of the dead body of her son at the foot of the cross, which some ancient spiritual writers referred to as Mary's "martyrdom." In both instances, Mary teaches us to *trust:* in God's wisdom, which so often contradicts the "evidence" about ourselves, and the "evidence" about the world and its fate. To enter into the mystery of the Blessed Virgin Mary is to take our first steps in the spiritual discipline of trust.

That trust extends beyond time to eternity. Mary, in Catholic teaching, is the first of disciples in every way: that is the meaning of the doctrine of the Assumption, which teaches that Mary was "assumed" body and soul into heaven, at her death—her "dormition," her "falling asleep." As she is the first of disciples at the beginning, so she is the first of disciples in the anticipation of what God intends for all of us: a bodily resurrection to eternal life forever, within the light and love of the Trinity. Here in the crypt of the Dormition Abbey, we are struck by the fact that there has never been a serious claim in Christian history, "Here is Mary" (as there is, for example, in the *scavi*: "Peter is here"). In the development of Catholic understanding, it took almost two thousand years to bring this intuition—that Mary must be the pattern of Christian discipleship *all the way*—to a formulation of doctrine; it only happened in 1950. But the trajectory was there from the beginning.

God's demonstration of his purposes for all of us is completed, in a sense, by the Assumption: here is *our* destiny because we, too, have been configured to Christ, the son of Mary and the Son of God. The Church teaches that the saints enjoy the fullness of God's life in heaven; but the saints, too, await the completion of God's saving purposes in the resurrection and transformation of their mortal bodies. *God saves all of us*, not just the "spiritual" within us. That is what the Catholic Church affirms in teaching the Assumption of Mary, the first of disciples in all things—the first to experience the fullness of that which awaits all the saved.

We might want to pray the rosary together here. The rosary has been the most popular form of Marian piety in the Catholic world for centuries. Praying the rosary fell out of favor in some Catholic circles in the years immediately after Vatican II, but the revival of the rosary in recent years tells us something important: the rosary is a privileged form of prayer precisely because it points us, through Mary, to the truth about her Son and the truths about us that he reveals and confirms.

For a very long time, the rosary was composed of fifteen "decades" (ten recitations of the Ave Maria, the prayer known as the Hail, Mary), each decade preceded by the Lord's Prayer and completed by a prayer to the Trinity. The fifteen decades, in turn, were clustered into three groups of five "mysteries": the Joyful Mysteries (involving events in the prepublic life of Christ), the Sorrowful Mysteries (the events of Christ's passion and death), and the Glorious Mysteries (the Resurrection and its effects in the life of the early Church). In 2002 Pope John Paul II surprised the Catholic world by suggesting that the Church add five new mysteries to the recitation of the rosary: the Luminous Mysteries or Mysteries of Light, recalling events in the public ministry of Christ—his baptism, the wedding at Cana and his first public miracle, the preaching of the kingdom, the transfiguration, the Last Supper and the institution of the Eucharist.

When I first heard that the Pope was "adding" mysteries to the rosary, I couldn't quite understand what he was up to. It seemed a bit odd: rather like adding extra innings to a baseball game. Shortly afterward, though, I found myself lecturing at a prestigious—and thoroughly, even aggressively, secular—college in the Northeast. After my lecture, a group of Catholic students invited me to the chapel they had set up and we prayed together the Luminous Mysteries. And I was sold. John Paul, it came clear to me, had filled a "gap" in the rosary. The traditional fifteen-decade rosary leaps from the late childhood of Christ (the last Joyful Mystery is the finding of the boy Jesus in the Temple) to the passion (the first Sorrowful Mystery being the Agony in the Garden). Something was missing—an opportunity to meet Christ, in the rosary, in his public life. The new Luminous Mysteries suggested by John Paul II are another opportunity to drink in the meaning of Mary's words at Cana—"Do whatever *he* tells you"—by reflecting through this rhythmic form of prayer on what Jesus did and said in five key moments of his ministry.

As my young friends at that college intuitively understood, the rosary is a prayer that lends itself well to reflection on *vocation*, on what it means to be called by God to a unique Christian mission. The first of the rosary's "mysteries"—the Annunciation—takes us back to Mary's *fiat* and reminds us that Mary as the first of disciples is also the pattern of Christian vocation. The Gospel tells us that Mary found the angel's greeting "troubling." And why not? But Mary's response amid her fears and doubts—Mary's *fiat*—vindicates the angel's greeting, that she is "full of grace." Mary doesn't negotiate. She doesn't ask for a prematernal contract, unlike today's couples with their "prenuptial agreements." Mary doesn't have an exit strategy. Mary doesn't "keep her options open." In fear and trembling, but with confidence in God's saving purposes, she gives the answer: *fiat*. Let it be. I am the Lord's servant and the Lord will provide.

"Keeping your options open" is not the path to happiness, wholeness—or holiness. That's an important Marian insight from the New Testament for every generation, but perhaps especially for yours. We've all heard, time and again, that yours is a generation "not ready to commit." Is that because yours is a generation short on trust? If so, it's not hard to understand why. You've seen the wreckage caused by the sexual revolution and its dissolution of trust between men and women, both within marriage and outside of it. You've seen public officials betray their oath of office, and priests and bishops betray the vows they swore to Christ and the Church at ordination. You've seen teachers and professors betray the truth because of expediency, cowardice, or an addiction to political correctness. If yours is a generation that finds it hard to trust and thus hard to "commit," that's understandable.

But not persuasive.

Perhaps this "trust deficit" is one of the reasons why so many young people found Pope John Paul II such a compelling figure. Here was commitment embodied in an irresistible way—particularly in the recent past, as the Pope's physical difficulties became, through his commitment, an instrument of preaching the Gospel of life and of God's powerful and transforming love. Unlike popular culture, the Pope didn't pander to you—he challenged you: never settle for less than the greatness of soul that God has made it possible for you to live, because of Christ. At the same time, he demonstrated with his life that he asked of you nothing that he hadn't asked of himself; he asked no commitment that he had not made, no struggle that he had not struggled through.

How could he do this? I think he gave the answer at Częstochowa, the great Polish shrine of the Black Madonna, Poland's most famous Marian icon, in 1979. There John Paul said, quite simply, "I am a man of great trust; I learned to be one here." I learned to trust here, in prayer before this image of Mary that draws us into the mystery of Mary's special role in salvation history—which is the world's history, read in its true depth. I learned to trust, not in "options" or "exit strategies," but in the mother who always points us toward her son, toward the Christ who never fails in his promises.

That's why the inclusion of the wedding feast at Cana in the new Luminous Mysteries of the rosary is another invitation to think and pray about your vocation. Every Catholic, every Christian, has a vocation—a unique *something* that only *you* can do in the providence of God. That, too, can be a disturbing thought—until we recognize that that same providence will, mercifully, repair and make straight whatever false steps we take in living out our vocational commitments. "Do whatever *he* tells you." That is Mary's message to us, as well as to the servants at the wedding feast in Cana. "Do whatever *he* tells you" is Mary's gentle invitation to make her *fiat* your own. Don't look for an "exit strategy." Live in trust, not in calculation; stake everything on Christ.

In his embrace, to which Mary points us, you'll find the path to happiness, wholeness, and holiness that you will never find by keeping your options open.

# 5

# The Oratory, Birmingham, England—Newman and "Liberal" Religion

In February 2003, I visited the famous Birmingham Oratory, founded by John Henry Newman in 1848. It's sometimes said, and not without reason, that Newman was the most important Catholic thinker of the past two centuries. The remarkable subtlety of Newman's theology (especially his thinking about the act of faith) is one facet of his enduring impact on contemporary Catholicism; his often exquisite prose is another. But even those who have a tough time working through the intellectual thickets of Newman's *Grammar of Assent* find the drama of his life and his conversions irresistible: the evangelical who made a brief tour into theological liberalism before becoming one of the leading lights of the "Tractarian" reform of High Church Anglicanism, a movement that eventually led him to Rome and, after no little trouble, a cardinal's red hat. The cause for Newman's beatification has been under way for decades and Newman has been declared "Venerable" by Pope John Paul II; the cause awaits a confirming miracle before the man whom some regard as the intellectual father of the Second Vatican Council becomes "Blessed John Henry Newman."

The Oratorians of Birmingham had kindly invited me to deliver the *laudatio*, a kind of keynote address, at their annual celebration of Newman's birthday, which falls on February 21. Founded by St. Philip Neri in Rome in 1564, the Oratory is one of those quirky curiosities that crop up throughout the Catholic world. Oratorians live in community but have no specific line of work as a founding purpose; they are very loosely organized, each Oratory being a virtually independent clerical kingdom. They typically combine genteel poverty with refined taste, a high-powered intellectual life, a fondness for good wine, and a minimum of creature comforts. As one of the Birmingham Oratorians led me to the guest room through somewhat musty corridors and showed me how to open the antique oak washstand near my bed (I couldn't tell whether the chamber pot had been hidden or retired), he said, quite cheerfully, "Walking through these halls gives you a real feeling for what it must have been like in the cardinal's day." To which I could only murmur in reply, "It certainly does."

The musical oratory in honor of Newman's 202nd birthday was a splendid affair in the beautiful Birmingham Oratory church (itself a sign of contradiction and hope in a neighborhood that's seen better days). My address was preceded and followed by wonderful music from the church's lay a cappella choir (singing pieces by Victoria, Stanford, and Mozart); a visiting string trio did a very nice job with Telemann's A-minor Sonata for Violin and Basso Continuo. Having begun with a hearty rendering of Newman's hymn, "Firmly I Believe and

Truly," we finished with an all-stops-pulled rendition of Newman's "Praise to the Holiest in the Height" before repairing en masse to the upper hall of the Oratory's cloister buildings, where a copious amount of Côtes du Rhône was drunk in honor of Newman and of our fellowship in honoring him.

The next morning, after a bracingly chilly night and a wrestling match with the oaken washstand, I came down to breakfast where the other side of English Oratorian life was on display. One of the fathers was served toast that was utterly black, burned to a fare-thee-well on all sides, and he munched happily on this bit of carbonized stale bread (smeared with a touch of marmalade) while reading his mail (in several languages) and, perhaps, contemplating his work as one of the Church's best translators of Latin into English: the Birmingham Oratory, you see, holds the civilized view that no man should be burdened with conversation that early in the morning. So talk is forbidden at breakfast, according to one of the Birmingham Oratory's delightfully odd rules.

All in all, as I told my wife, it was rather like stepping into a cartoon from *Punch*, sometime in the last quarter of the nineteenth century. What *Punch* would have satirized, though, seemed more like interesting, even holy, eccentricity to me.

Which is an entirely appropriate ambiance in which to ponder Newman, a great hero of Catholic "progressives" who spent much of his intellectual life combating what he called "liberal religion," and what he might mean for you.

Newman's rooms and library are preserved at the Birmingham Oratory just as he left them when he died, at age eighty-nine, on August 11, 1890. And when I say "just as he left them," I mean that quite literally. With Father Dermot Fenlon of the Oratory as my guide, I could sit at Newman's small desk, finger his rosary beads, examine the Latin breviaries he and his friend Hurrell Froude had used as Anglicans (causing great scandal). On the wall to my left was a faded clip from one of the London newspapers: a map of Egypt and Sudan, tracing General Kitchener's path to Khartoum, where he was supposed to rescue General Gordon. Someone had, evidently, gotten word to Newman that Gordon, besieged in Khartoum by the wild-eyed forces of the Mahdi, was preparing for death by reading Newman's lengthy poem, *The Dream of Gerontius*. Behind me was the small fireplace at which the aged cardinal tried to take the chill from his bones before retiring for the night, aided by a glass or two of brandy (and the glasses are still there, too).

Getting up from the desk and walking around a bookcase that separates the sitting room from a small chapel, I could open the door of an antique wardrobe to find Newman's red hat, the cardinal's gallero, complete with tassels, propped up against the back wall. The altar is still set as if for Mass; the walls behind and on both sides of it are covered with notes and cards, pinned in place by Newman to remind him of the people for whom he had promised to pray.

In another part of the Oratory, a small band of devoted archivists are systematically organizing, editing, annotating, and publishing Newman's vast correspondence and his diaries, one thick volume at a time. The most recent editor of the series, Gerard Tracey, had died just a month before my visit. With long, flowing gray locks that hung past his shoulders, this meticulous scholar looked like nothing so much as one of the elves in *The Lord of the Rings*; the Oratorians, with a fine sense of the appropriate, buried a layman who had devoted his entire working life to Newman near the cardinal in their graveyard at Rednal. In this workspace, you can, quite literally, touch Newman's work, thanks to the labors of men like Gerard Tracey: pull the box marked "Apologia" from the shelf and you can read through the originals of Newman's correspondence with his publisher about his extraordinary spiritual autobiography, perhaps the only one in Christian history worthy to be mentioned in the same breath as Augustine's *Confessions*.

It's all as if it were . . . today. And that feeling is intensified when you open another wardrobe in the archivists' workshop and find Newman's cardinalatial robes, which he may have worn only once in his life, when he sat for the famous portrait by Sir John Millais that's now in the National Portrait Gallery in London. Or, if you like, pick up and try on one of the two or three cardinal's birettas that rest in the same wardrobe.

It's in Newman's library, though, that Newman "lives" most powerfully—or so it seemed to me. The library is a large, high-ceilinged horseshoe, with an iron catwalk that allows you access to the books shelved on the second tier. Go to the left, on the first tier, and take out the large white folio volume of the *Opera Omnia*, the collected works, of St. Gregory the Great: there, on the flyleaf, you'll find a dedication of this gift to Newman from his friend and fellow Tractarian, Edward Pusey, in Pusey's own hand. Turning around, you see a stand-up desk; here, in the white heat of controversy, Newman wrote the *Apologia pro Vita Sua*, his spiritual autobiography, in a mere two months—tears, Father Dermot tells you, falling onto the pages as he wrote. (Charles Kingsley, an Anglican divine and writer, had accused Newman, and the Catholic clergy in general, of dishonesty—of being willing to dissemble, even lie, without any qualms of conscience, if that served the interests of the Church. Newman's devastatingly effective response in the *Apologia* demolished Kingsley's reputation, a fact that Kingsley never quite seemed to understand.)

Newman could be precious, bordering on vain, and he was adept at satirical polemic; the subtleties of his thought could be taken by less intelligent readers (like Charles Kingsley) as dissembling or evasion; the originality of his mind could strike the guardians of a brittle form of Catholic orthodoxy as dangerously innovative, perhaps even heretical. So it was no wonder that Newman's entire adult life was spent in controversy—often bitter controversy. In addition to Kingsley's attack, Newman was long held suspect by Catholics who, in the old saw, imagined themselves more Catholic than the pope.

Newman believed that the pope could, under certain well-defined circumstances, infallibly define matters of faith and morals. Given the intellectual, political, and ecumenical circumstances of the second half of the nineteenth century, however, he wondered whether it was prudent to assert this truth through the action of an ecumenical council. This put Newman into conflict with a former friend and fellow convert from Anglicanism, Henry Edward Manning, archbishop of Westminster and one of the chief lobbyists for defining papal infallibility at Vatican I (1869–1870). The council eventually affirmed the doctrine, which, despite the moderation of its formulation, prompted a sharp public attack on

Catholicism by William Gladstone, the former prime minister and one of the great political figures of the day. Newman's defense of the doctrine against Gladstone, in his *Letter to the Duke of Norfolk*, was much more effective, among both Anglicans and Catholics, than Manning's. Yet Newman fell again under a Roman shadow when a bad translation of the *Letter* prompted yet another round of questions about his orthodoxy. In 1879, however, the new pope, Leo XIII, created him a cardinal and permitted him to remain at the Birmingham Oratory (in those days, cardinals who were not residential bishops were required to live in Rome). Newman's vindication was at hand. He made the most of the occasion, thereby leaving all of us with something to think about.

---

Despite his age (he was 78 at the time), Newman traveled to Rome to receive the red hat—the one that's still in the wardrobe in his rooms—from the hands of Pope Leo XIII. There, on May 12, 1879, he delivered an address in which he said that "for thirty, forty, fifty years I have resisted to the best of my powers the spirit of liberalism in religion." What did Newman mean by "liberalism?" The *Apologia* contains a long "Note" in which Newman spelled out eighteen "liberal" propositions which he "earnestly denounced and abjured." They're worth your reading—indeed, the entire *Apologia* is worth your reading—but, for the moment, let's stick with Newman's Roman address of 1879, when he gave a more concise account of what it was that he had been fighting against for decades:

> *Liberalism in religion is the doctrine that there is no positive truth in religion, but that one creed is as good as another, and this is the teaching which is gaining force and substance daily. It is inconsistent with any recognition of any religion, as true. It teaches that all are to be tolerated, for all are matters of opinion. Revealed religion is not a truth, but a sentiment and a taste; not an objective fact, not miraculous; and it is the right of each individual to make it say just what strikes his fancy. Devotion is not necessarily founded on faith. Men may go to Protestant Churches and to Catholic, may get good from both and belong to neither. They may fraternize together in spiritual thoughts and feelings, without having any views at all of doctrine in common, or seeing the need of them.*

Newman's enemies accused him of emotional instability and intellectual shiftiness, citing his several conversions as evidence. Newman thought of his life as of a piece: when he was converted to evangelical Anglicanism from a brief adolescent experiment in atheism; when his evangelicalism gave way to a dalliance with liberal Anglicanism; when dissatisfaction with the liberal camp led him to High Church Anglicanism and the Tractarian movement; when his historical research and theological reflection as a Tractarian led him to the conclusion that the Catholic Church was in fact what it claimed to be—the embodiment of the apostolic Church willed by Christ. All of this, in Newman's mind, fit together. He was embarked on a great spiritual journey that had led him from willfulness to obedience; from a skepticism answerable only to his own judgments to a conviction that there were truths God had revealed to which *we* were accountable; from the loneliness (and pridefulness) of doing things and believing things *my* way to the sometimes difficult but ultimately consoling conviction that a God who had revealed himself would have also given the world a vessel in which the truth of that revelation would be preserved and defended—the Catholic Church. Newman was no romantic about the Catholic Church; he knew all about its weaknesses and flaws, and he suffered repeatedly at the hands of Catholic incompetents and heresy hunters. But he read his own life, and his journey into Catholicism, in the terms he asked to have inscribed on his tombstone: *Ex umbris et imaginibus in veritatem* (From shadows and appearances into truth).

Catholicism, he insisted, is not a matter of *opinion* but *truth*. "Liberal" Catholicism, like every other form of "liberal" Christianity, was its own worst enemy, in Newman's view. "Liberal" religion had no internal brake, no way of saying, "Here is where opinion stops and truth begins." It had no mechanism to keep itself from unraveling, from changing itself to the point where there was no self left. "Liberal" religion couldn't tell the difference between appearances and reality, shadows and the truth of things.

That's as true today as it was in Newman's day. And it's just as hard a saying today as it was then—perhaps harder.

We live in a culture saturated by what Newman called "liberalism"—a culture in which about all that can be conceded is that there may be *your* truth and *my* truth, what's good for you and what's good for me. To assert that there might be something properly described as *the* truth is not only considered odd, it's usually considered intolerant. In a culture that values "tolerance" (or what it imagines to be tolerance) above all else, to be called "intolerant" is about as bad as it gets. Newman's life and work suggest it's a risk worth taking—*if* you understand that genuine tolerance means engaging differences with respect and civility, not in avoiding differences as if they made no difference; *if* you're interested in traveling *ex umbris et imaginibus*—from shadows and appearances—into the light. Newman's life and work remind us that the quest for truth is one of the greatest of human quests—*if* we understand that the purpose of the journey is not the journey itself but getting to the destination, which is the light.

To stand with Newman against "liberal" religion is emphatically *not* to stand against questioning and probing and developing our understanding, and the Church's understanding, of the truth. Newman's was a modern mind. He knew about skepticism, having lived in it and with it. He had no use for forms of Catholic philosophy and theology that reduced the faith and its truths to a series of coldly logical deductions. He was a thinker from the bottom up, so to speak, rather than from the top down. And because of that, he knew that questions and questioning were essential to mature faith. Catholic faith, he understood, was not a matter of saying yes to truth in the same way that we say yes to the truth that two plus two always equals four in the base-ten system. The act of faith was richer, more complex than that. In the *Grammar of Assent*, his most technically difficult work and a marvel of finely honed distinctions in its exploration of the religious mind, he coined a phrase, the "illative sense," to describe how a convergence of factors reaches a point where probabilities, added together, drive us to certainties. This can be so powerful a force within us that it functions like a proof, even though it isn't a proof strictly speaking.

Let's try to see what Newman was driving at through another conversion story. In the summer of 1921, Edith Stein, a brilliant young German philosopher who as a teenager had abandoned her parents' Judaism, was wrestling with questions of faith. She was spending a few days with some Lutheran friends, fellow philosophers, who had to go out of an evening. Edith Stein stayed at their home and, looking for something to read, pulled the *Autobiography* of St. Teresa of Avila out of her hosts' library. She got no sleep that night. At dawn, she finished reading and said, simply, "This is the truth." She then went out to buy a catechism and a missal. Four months or so later, she was baptized. Twenty-one years later, as a Carmelite nun, she was martyred in the gas chambers of Auschwitz. Edith Stein was canonized on October 11, 1998, under her Carmelite name, Saint Teresa Benedicta of the Cross.

One of Edith Stein's biographers sums up her conversion, and its "trigger" in her reading of St. Teresa's *Autobiography*, like this: "So convinced was she of the truth of St. Teresa's experience that she had to acknowledge the source of that experience as Truth itself." Here is Newman's "illative sense" at work. But don't get blocked by that strange phrase. Think of what Newman was talking about, and what Edith Stein experienced, as a form of *grace*, mediated through powerful human experiences. In this sense, God's grace does for the believer what "genius" does for the artist or the theoretical physicist. It *brings things together* in so powerful a way that the force of the truth demands a response, an affirmation, a "yes." Even if, as for Newman, that conversion leads to broken friendships, loss of career, loneliness, and controversy; even if, as for Edith Stein, that conversion leads to martyrdom.

What does all this have to do with Newman's polemic against "liberal" religion? Everything. "Liberal" religion creates what the Jewish scholar David Gelernter calls an "ice-your-own-cupcake world," because "liberal" religion is religion-we-make-up. *Revealed* religion, on the other hand, is religion-into-which-we-are-incorporated. Liberal religion has no confidence in the human capacity to be seized by the truth of things—by a saving word of revelation from the God of Abraham, Isaac, Jacob, Moses, and Jesus: a *God who reveals himself*, not propositions about himself. Mature Catholic faith is a matter of being seized by the truth in such a way that we *know*, in a special way of knowing, that, as Edith Stein said in Hedwig Conrad-Martius's guest room, "This is the truth." It's not something we invent. It's not something we can buy. It's something we can only receive. It's a gift, a gift that demands a response.

And the name of that response, to be even more countercultural, is *obedience*. Not childish servitude. Mature *obedience*. Courageous obedience. John Henry Newman described the special joy of this obedience to revealed truth in one of his novels:

> *Certainty, in its highest sense, is the reward of those who, by an act of will, and at the dictate of reason and prudence, embrace the truth, when nature, like a coward, shrinks [from it]. You must make a venture; faith is a venture before a man is a Catholic; it is a gift after it. You approach the*

*Church in the way of reason, you enter it in the light of the Spirit.*

As you consider what it means to be a Catholic today, here's one of the things you must wrestle with: liberal Christianity is dying. When the legitimate questioning, probing, and developing that are essential for theology erode into religion-we-make-up, Christian communities decay. For there seems to be an iron law built into the Christian encounter with modern life and culture: Christian communities that maintain a clear sense of their doctrinal and moral borders flourish, while Christian communities whose borders become so porous that it's hard to tell who's in and who's out wither and die. Even a cursory examination of the demographics of world Christianity bears this out.

That iron law is as true within Catholicism as it is in the wider Christian world. Just as liberal Protestantism is dying today, a century and a half after Newman diagnosed the lethal disease that beset it, so is what often calls itself "liberal" or "progressive" Catholicism. It's not an accident that the Catholic Church is flourishing where the Second Vatican Council is understood to be a bracing affirmation of Christian orthodoxy and where the adventure of orthodoxy is understood to be the greatest of human adventures. It's not an accident that religious orders and seminaries that take seriously the distinctive mission, way of life, and dress of religious life and the priesthood are growing, while self-consciously liberal religious orders and seminaries are dying. It's not an accident that the fastest growing lay renewal movements are those that take the hardest demands of

Catholic life most seriously. And it's no accident that the Church is in deep, deep trouble in those parts of western Europe, Canada, and Oceania where the romance of orthodoxy has been displaced by the siren songs of what Newman described as "liberal" religion: of Christianity understood as opinion, or hobby, or lifestyle choice, not truth. Catholic Lite, as I've called it, has no real future.

For the better part of forty years, ever since Vatican II, the Catholic story has been presented in the media (and, truth to tell, in a lot of the Church) as a story of "good" liberals versus "bad" conservatives. To get identified with the latter—even if the term "conservative" makes no sense in describing people who, within the boundaries of orthodoxy, are exploring the frontiers of Catholic faith in a thoroughly modern way—is to find yourself in the crosshairs of the culture and the crosshairs of Catholic liberals for whom everything is to be tolerated except those dreadful conservatives (much less neoconservatives!). And that can get very uncomfortable.

It's worth it, though. At the same time, when we stand up for the great adventure of orthodoxy, we always have to remember Flannery O'Connor's injunction against Catholic smugness. So always remember that there are many, many Catholics who, according to the regnant categories, think of themselves as good *liberal* Catholics, just as there are bishops who believe that the function of religious leadership is to "walk straight down the middle," as one prominent American prelate put it, "touching both sides as you go." It's not our role to question the commitment of obviously committed Catholics (although it may be our role, on occasion, to challenge both ourselves and our liberal friends to a deeper fidelity and a more radical commitment). And yes, that bishop was on to something when he told his seminarians that he wanted them to be in touch with everybody in the Church, not just the people they agreed with.

But remember, too, that you can't split the difference quite so neatly as that. John Henry Newman staked his life on the judgment that liberal religion and revealed religion aren't two forms of the same thing; they're two different things. Too much of what calls itself "liberal Catholicism" today is very much like what Newman described in his 1879 polemic against liberalism: sentiment and taste rather than revealed religion. That it hasn't got much of a future seems pretty clear from the demographics. But that's not the real problem. The real problem, as Newman understood, is that this kind of liberalism deprives us of the joy that can only come from the obedience of faith.

---

I have to confess that it took me a while to accept this. Perhaps a brief outline of the story of how it happened will be of some interest to you as you consider your own position.

When I studied theology in college and graduate school, in the heady years just after the Second Vatican Council, we really thought that we could, and should, reinvent the Catholic world. In that atmosphere (which was, of course, deeply influenced by currents in the wider culture), the "obedience of faith" was not a phrase you regularly encountered. We didn't spend very much time considering Newman's critique of "liberal religion." Modernity was standing in judgment on doctrine;

doctrine wasn't the standard by which we were to judge modernity. Everything seemed plastic and malleable, and we were filled with an exhilarating sense of living on the cutting edge of the Catholic future.

I vividly remember a party that, in retrospect, captured the temper of those times. One of my professors, an official theological adviser (or *peritus*) at Vatican II and a founder of *Concilium*, the international journal of self-consciously "progressive" theology, regaled us with council stories: machinations over getting draft texts of council documents secretly printed, various theological and political plots, back-channel negotiations. It was, he memorably said, a "theologians' paradise." At the time, it sounded like a terrific description (and experience) to me, because I had absorbed the conventional story line and assumed he was referring to the council as a great contest of ideas, a Catholic Waterloo or Gettysburg at which theologians who had long been squashed by Roman bureaucrats were vindicated in their efforts to bring the Catholic Church into dialogue with the modern world.

To give my old teacher the benefit of the doubt, I think that is what he thought he was describing: a contest of ideas, in which people who believed in the vitality of ideas had won. In his own way, I'm sure he understood that struggle to be a struggle for the truth. (Even if he once summed up his basic theological position in these rather lame terms: "That God is alive means that tomorrow will be different from today"—which is not exactly what Edith Stein found in the *Autobiography* of Teresa of Avila.) At the same time, my professor was also talking, if unconsciously, about power: Vatican II had been a "paradise" for many theologians because it was their first, enticing taste of power. To be sure, distinguished theologians helped the bishops craft the many fine documents of the Second Vatican Council. While they were doing that, though, some of these intellectuals also came to think of themselves as a new form of teaching authority in the Church. And what they were promoting through that self-validating authority was, by and large, what John Henry Newman would have called "liberal" religion. Go to most Catholic theology departments in the United States today, and you'll find a lot of it on tap, at least among professors over fifty.

I started questioning the liberal Catholic project when I left graduate school and started teaching and writing—two activities that force you to think through what you really think. Native contrariness probably played some role in my intellectual journey away from Catholic liberalism; by the same token, I can say in all honesty that I found the two great enthusiasms of those years—liberation theology and feminist theology—intellectually shallow and unsatisfying. In college and graduate school, the influential German theologian Karl Rahner, who dominated "liberal" Catholic theology for decades, had been my lodestar. Well do I remember the night when, after reading the tedious prologue to Rahner's *Foundations of Christian Faith*, which described the modern crisis of belief, something suddenly dawned on me—"I don't know anyone he's talking about." And I began to think that a theology whose primary reference point was the contemporary academy and its profound nervousness about the very idea of "truth" was not going to be of much interest beyond the seminar room. My fondness for history was probably another factor in getting me to embrace Newman's critique of liberalism. Because I have always been excited by history, I suppose the liberal tendency to dismiss the past as largely irrelevant to contemporary concerns finally grated on me once too often.

A lot of my discontents with the categories in which I had been intellectually trained came into clearer focus in the late 1970s, when I read an ecumenical broadside called "An Appeal for Theological Affirmation," which was widely known as the Hartford Appeal. Its signatories included some of the most influential religious thinkers in North America, only a few of whom would—in those days, at least—have welcomed being described as "conservatives." Yet, as I remember it, the Hartford Appeal had been mocked in my graduate school as the Hartford Heresies and dismissed as a matter of "good liberals" losing their nerve. On closer examination, and through the prism of my new skepticism about liberal Catholic shibboleths, a much more interesting picture came into focus—in their own way, the signatories of the Hartford Appeal were bringing John Henry Newman's critique of liberal religion up to date. Newman got it exactly right in his *Apologia* with its appended note on liberalism. The real issue was not "liberals versus conservatives," but rather liberal religion versus revealed religion.

What case did the Hartford Appeal make?

It began by challenging the view that "modern thought is superior to all past forms of understanding reality," such that "modern thought" stands in judgment on classic Christian doctrine and practice. Rather, Christian thinking should adopt an ecumenism of time, employing wisdom and insight from any historical era.

The Hartford signatories argued against the suggestion that "religious language refers to human experience and nothing else." Why? Because if that's the case, then God is "humanity's noblest invention." With Newman, the Hartford Appeal insisted, "*We did not invent God; God invented us.*"

Again with Newman, the Hartford Appeal denied that "all religions are equally valid," with its corollary that "the choice among them is not a matter of . . . truth but only of personal preference or lifestyle." Christianity reduced to a lifestyle choice is Christianity emptied of its power.

Salvation, the Hartford signatories affirmed, includes a "promise of human fulfillment." But it is false to suggest that "to realize one's potential and to be true to oneself is the whole meaning of salvation." God's promises are not to be trivialized, and God promises more than the "human fulfillment" that psychobabble imagines. By the same token, the Hartford Appeal insisted that, while worship is personally and communally enriching, it's a fundamental mistake to assume that the only purposes of worship are "self-realization and human community." Worship is a response to God's initiative. We do not worship God because it makes us feel good or more connected; "we worship God because God is to be worshiped," and doing so arises out of the fundamental human "desire to know, love, and adore God."

The Hartford signatories flatly denied that "the world sets the agenda for the Church" (a theme then being promoted by the World Council of Churches), and insisted that Christian social action, which was imperative, must be informed by distinctively Christian understandings of the world. Moreover, the appeal insisted, it was precisely because of their confidence in God's transcendence—"God's reign over all aspects of life"—that Christians could engage in the fray against all forms of human oppression. To identify God's reign with any mundane political or economic program was idolatry because "God has his own designs which confront ours, surprising us with judgment and redemption."

Why revisit the Hartford Appeal, which is almost thirty years old? Read it as an invitation to Newman and his critique of liberal religion. Hartford's language may be a little more accessible than Newman's, which takes some getting used to; and Hartford's reference points, in the Church and the world, are all around us, unlike Newman's. Remember, though, that Newman and the Hartford signatories saw the same great truth: that *obedience to Christian truth is liberating* in the deepest sense of human liberation. That truth comes from God and invites us to a personal encounter with God through Jesus Christ and his Church. It's not something we make up for ourselves. It's something we can only receive as a gift.

Cherish it for the great gift it is.

6

# The Olde Cheshire Cheese, London—Chesterton's Pub and a Sacramental World

The "Catholic world" has a lot more to it than churches. It's also a world of libraries and bedrooms, mountains and the seaside, galleries and sports fields, concert halls and monastic cells—places where we get glimpses and hints of the extraordinary that lies just on the far side of the ordinary (to borrow from Alfred North Whitehead, who wasn't a Catholic but had a Catholic sensibility in this respect). That's why I want to take you to a pub, the Olde Cheshire Cheese, on London's Fleet Street. One of the great Catholic troubadours of the world and its sacramentality, Gilbert Keith Chesterton, spent more than a few evenings here. We should pay it a visit, too.

The dark wooden interiors of the Olde Cheshire Cheese have seen a lot of English literary history. Samuel Johnson used to hold forth here, as only he could; his house was a few steps away, and according to some accounts he was in the Cheese daily. So, we may assume, was his biographer, Boswell. Dryden, Thackeray, and Dickens were all regulars in their day. As we go into the pub from a narrow alley, Wine Office Court, you'll cross a metal grate that protects the old stone step at the entrance. Once upon a time, before the grate was in place to protect this third-class relic, you could walk into the Cheshire Cheese in the footsteps, literally, of some of the greats of English literature. Now for the first-floor bar. The portrait over the fireplace is of one William Simpson, a waiter who served the Cheshire Cheese and its distinguished clientele in the first third of the nineteenth century. Dickens's favorite drinking table is the one to the right of the fireplace.

Had you come to the Cheese in the early twentieth century, you might well have had the luck to find G. K. Chesterton, often with his brother Cecil and their friend Hilaire Belloc: three men convinced that the truths God wants us to find in this world were to be found, not only in churches and lecture halls, but in places like the Olde Cheshire Cheese—places that provided the good food and good drink that enabled good fellowship and good conversation. Imagine Belloc at the table, regaling his friends with stories of his 1906 campaign for Parliament in South Salford, where Belloc's Conservative Party opponents had adopted the bigoted slogan, "Don't vote for a Frenchman and a Catholic" (Belloc's father was French). Never one to duck an argument, Belloc deliberately chose a Catholic school for his first campaign speech. The local priests advised him to avoid the issue of his faith; Belloc was having none of it. The hall was packed and he pulled no punches: "Gentlemen, I am a Catholic. As far as possible, I go to Mass every day. This is a rosary. As far as possible, I kneel down and tell these beads every day. If you reject me on account of my religion, I shall thank God that He has spared me the indignity of being your representative." The workers of South Salford gave him a standing ovation and elected him a few weeks later. G. K. Chesterton, who wouldn't become a Catholic for another sixteen years, would have roared his approval and then, perhaps, wiped the tears of laughter off his ample face. Here were men who knew, as Belloc biographer Joseph Pearce once put it, that "love and laughter were linked in a mystical unity," because "beyond the mere love of laughter was to be found the laughter of love."

All of which makes it entirely appropriate that the Olde Cheshire Cheese stands today, as it did in the days of what Londoners used to call the "Chesterbelloc," on the site of a thirteenth-century Carmelite monastery. There are "Catholic places" and then there are "Catholic places"—and some of them are recycled, so to speak, in different livery in different centuries.

But I digress. On to Chesterton.

An English friend once said of Theodore Roosevelt, "You must always remember that the President is about six." G. K. Chesterton (or "GKC," as he signed his journalism) was always about five. Born in 1874, he had not lost a child's fascination with the world when he died, at sixty-two, in 1936. Through religious struggles, the hard grind of journalism, political controversies, and intellectual combat, GKC retained a five-year-old's wonder at the world around him and at the people he met, loved, ate, drank, and argued with. The *Encyclopedia Britannica*, after listing his credits as "English critic and author of verse, essays, novels, and short stories," remarks that Chesterton was "known also for his exuberant personality and rotund figure." At first blush, it can seem a rather odd description for a literary genius who was a respectable amateur theologian and a first-rate Christian apologist. But, with GKC, what you see is what you get: the manner of the man spoke volumes about his conviction that the human comedy is, in the deepest sense, a divine comedy.

---

We've spoken before about the bedrock Catholic conviction that *stuff counts*. Chesterton fervently believed that, although it took him until age fifty-two to enter into full communion with the Catholic Church. Thus, even in his pre-Catholic years, GKC was an ardent defender of the *sacramental imagination*—the core Catholic conviction that God saves and sanctifies the world through the materials of the world. You've probably heard it said that Catholicism is uneasy in the world, that Catholicism demeans the world and the flesh. Don't believe it for a second.

Catholicism takes the world, and the things of the world, far more seriously than those who like to think of themselves as worldly. Water, salt, and oil are the tangibles by which sanctifying grace is conferred in the *sacrament* of baptism; bread and wine are the materials through which Christ gives his body and blood to his people in the *sacrament* of the Eucharist; in the *sacrament* of matrimony, the consummation of marital love completes the vows exchanged at a Catholic couple's wedding; oil brings healing in the *sacrament* of the Anointing of the Sick, as it conveys the gift of the Holy Spirit in the *sacrament* of Confirmation. None of this happens by Harry Potter–like wizardry, but *because the world was sacramentally configured by God "in the beginning"* (cf. Genesis 1:1)—*and still is today* (cf. everything around you). What we experience here in what skeptics call the "real world" is a window into the *really* real world that makes this world possible, the world of transcendent Truth and Love. The ordinary stuff of the world is the material God uses to bring us into communion with the truly extraordinary—with God himself.

The ancient enemy of this sacramental imagination is what we might call the *gnostic imagination*. Gnosticism, one of the first Christian heresies, is remarkably resilient, even protean. It crops up time and again, generation after generation, in slightly different guises and disguises: from the Manichees who once seduced Augustine, through the medieval Albigensians and Cathari, and down to the present. Whenever and however it appears, though, gnosticism teaches the same seductive and devastating message: stuff *doesn't* count; the material world is a distraction (even a wicked distraction); what counts is the *gnosis*, the arcane knowledge, that lifts the elect, the elite, out of the grubbiness of the quotidian. Gnosticism can't handle the Incarnation—the truth that God enters the world in the person of his Son, the Second Person of the Trinity, to redeem and sanctify us *in* our humanity, not to fetch us out of it. And God does that because, as in the beginning, God understands that his creation is *good*, even *very good* (Genesis 1:31). Because gnosticism can't accept the goodness of the world, it can't "get" the Incarnation, and it can't accept the sacraments. Whether it appears in ancient guise or modern dress, gnosticism is the polar opposite of Catholic earthiness. It's also, invariably, elitist.

As far as I know, Chesterton never used the terms "sacramental imagination" and "gnostic imagination." But the former is what he passionately defended, and the latter is what he passionately criticized. Chesterton's genius was in seeing the devilishly clever turn taken by the modern gnostic imagination: it demeans the material through the guise of materialism. Let me take you on a tour of Chesterton's analysis and argument by way of some of my favorite Chestertonisms, drawn from his small book, *Orthodoxy*, published thirteen years before he entered the Catholic Church.

---

### *On the Right Kind of Worldliness*

*Thoroughly worldly people never understand even the world; they rely altogether on a few cynical maxims that are not true.*

Here is GKC's master indictment: a worldliness closed in on itself misses the full truth of the world. Worldliness is no bad thing, if by "worldliness" we mean taking seriously the stuff of the world, most especially including the lives and loves, passions and commitments of ordinary, unexceptional people. But that's not what modern worldliness does. For self-consciously "worldly" moderns, usually found in elite circles, *nothing* counts. Everything is ephemera; everything is plastic, changeable, manipulable. (Think of the more delirious forms of feminism, which insist that biology counts for nothing and means nothing, maleness and femaleness being cultural constructs. Or think of the Freudian reduction of the human condition to *sola psyche*.) The wrong kind of worldliness thinks of the world as a closed house without windows or doors; nothing in the house's layout or decoration is of very much consequence, except as it bears on transient pleasures. GKC's world, by contrast, is an open house with windows, doors, and skylights. The light illuminates the givenness of the things in the house, helping us see that what's given is full of meaning (like maleness and femaleness and their interrelation).

---

### *On Why We Need Our Imaginations*

*Imagination does not breed insanity. Exactly what does breed insanity is reason. Poets do not go mad; but chess-players do. Mathematicians go mad, and cashiers; but creative artists very seldom. I am not . . . in any sense attacking logic: I only say that this danger does lie in logic, not in imagination. . . . To accept everything is an exercise, to understand everything is a strain. The poet only desires exaltation and expansion, a world to stretch himself in. The poet only asks to get his head into the heavens. It is the logician who seeks to get the heavens into his head. And it is his head that splits.*

Here's another lesson in the sacramental imagination. To reduce what we can "know" to what we can rationally "prove" is dehumanizing—and it's another deprecation of the world and its sacramentality. You can't "prove" the "truth" to be found in friendship or love, in intellectual or political or spiritual passion, in Mozart's

"Prague" Symphony, in Rachmaninoff's *Vespers*—or in hitting the low outside corner with a 90 m.p.h. slider. But these "truths" exist, and they give life not only its tang but its meaning. To deny the truth of these things is to lock oneself into the prison of a windowless world. It's stifling. And you'll eventually suffocate. Chesterton argued that a lot of the modern world was dying of suffocation. Look at the history of the twentieth century, and see if you don't think he had a pretty strong case.

---

***On Small and Large Infinities***

*The madman is not the man who has lost his reason. The madman is the man who has lost everything except his reason . . . his mind moves in a perfect but narrow circle. A small circle is quite as infinite as a large circle; but, though it is quite as infinite, it is not so large . . . There is such a thing as a narrow universality; there is such a thing as a small and cramped eternity . . . [The] strongest and most unmistakable mark of madness is this combination between a logical completeness and a spiritual contraction.*

What's wrong with the way many skeptical moderns "see" the world? They see the world as a narrow infinity, because they've lost a sense of sacramentality. As GKC put it, the modern materialist skeptic—the modern gnostic—"understands everything, and everything does not seem worth understanding." Catholicism offers a different kind of infinity: a larger infinity, in which reason is enriched by imagination and imagination is disciplined by reason. As I already suggested, in the Catholic sacramental imagination, we "think" with our brains, our senses, and our emotions. Thinking with only our brains gives us a headache; it also gives us an aching soul. The deepest longings within us—for communion with others, wisdom, joy, accomplishment, love—cannot be satisfied by reducing the world to syllogisms. Human beings were made for a wider infinity, for a more ample eternity.

---

### *On Our Need for Mystery*

*Mysticism keeps men sane. As long as you have mystery you have health; when you destroy mystery you create morbidity. The ordinary man has always been sane because the ordinary man has always been a mystic. He has permitted the twilight. He always has one foot in earth and the other in fairyland. He has always left himself free to doubt his gods; but (unlike the agnostic today) free also to believe in them . . . The whole secret of mysticism is this: that a man can understand everything by the help of what he does not understand. The morbid logician seeks to make everything lucid, and succeeds in making everything mysterious. The mystic allows one thing to be mysterious, and everything else becomes lucid.*

When GKC says "mysticism" here, I think what he's getting at is the sacramental imagination—the experience of the extraordinary through the ordinary. That's the mysticism to which every Catholic is called. The "dark night" mysticism of St. John of the Cross is not a universal experience; neither is the burning mystical exaltation Bernini captured in marble in his *Ecstasy of St. Teresa of Avila*. The "mysticism" available to every Catholic is the experience of a world open to the transcendent. That's why, for Chesterton, the cross is the most apt of Catholic symbols. A circle, he wrote, suggests perfection and infinity, but a perfection "fixed for ever in its size." The cross, by comparison, "has at its heart a collision and a contradiction." Precisely because of that it "can extend its four arms forever without altering its shape. Because it has a paradox in its center it can grow without changing. The circle returns in upon itself and is bound. The cross opens its arms to the four winds; it is a signpost for free travelers."

---

### *On Tradition*

*Tradition may be defined as the extension of the franchise. Tradition means giving votes to the most obscure of all classes, our ancestors. It is the democracy of the dead. Tradition refuses to submit to the small and arrogant oligarchy of those who merely happen to be walking about. All democrats object to men being disqualified by the accident of birth;*

*tradition objects to their being disqualified by the accident of death. Democracy tells us not to neglect a good man's opinion, even if he is our groom; traditions asks us not to neglect a good man's opinion, even if he is our father.*

Or our grandfather. Or our great-grandmother's great-grandmother. Because the gnostic imagination can't take the world with the true seriousness it deserves, modern gnostics have little use for the past: everything has to be recreated anew, over and over again. In a sacramentally configured world, by contrast, the past counts—not because of nostalgia but because of reverence. Because it's part of this sacramentally configured world, what was lived and learned in the past can also be for us a window into the truth, beauty, and goodness of things here and now. And that's another dimension of authentically Catholic liberation: we don't have to make it up for ourselves. We can stand on the shoulders of spiritual and intellectual giants, and can see all the more clearly from that vantage point.

---

### On Optimism and Pessimism

*When I was a boy there were two curious men running about who were called the optimist and the pessimist. I constantly used the words myself, but I cheerfully confess that I never had any very special*

> *idea of what they meant. . . . Upon the whole, I came to the conclusion that the optimist thought everything good except the pessimist, and the pessimist thought everything bad, except himself.*

A little later in his ruminations on optimism and pessimism, GKC suggests that the choice between them is false because both assume that "a man criticizes this world as if he were house-hunting, as if he were being shown over a new suite of apartments." But no one, he continues, is in that position: "A man belongs to this world before he begins to ask if it is nice to belong to it. . . . My acceptance of the universe is not optimism, it is more like patriotism. . . . The world is not a lodging-house at Brighton, which we are to leave because it is miserable. It is the fortress of our family, with the flag flying on the turret, and the more miserable it is the less we should leave it. The point is not that this world is too sad to love or too glad not to love; the point is that when you do love a thing, its gladness is a reason for loving it, and its sadness a reason for loving it more." That's a *sacramental* appreciation of the world. Today's gnostics, for whom nothing really counts, can be optimists or pessimists because optimism and pessimism are mere matters of optics, of how you look at things, and that can change from day to day, or with a new prescription for your glasses—or with a new set of ideological filters. (It's no accident that the post–9/11 political commentaries of a premier modern gnostic, the French critic Jacques Derrida, have been notable for their utter incoherence, even meaninglessness.) In the sacramental imagination, which teaches us a profound loyalty to the world and how it's been made, we're neither optimists nor pessimists. As Catholics, we're men and women of *hope*—a far sturdier thing than optimism; hope is a virtue that rests on another virtue, faith.

---

### *On Laughter, or Why Satan Fell*

*Seriousness is not a virtue. It would be a heresy, but a much more sensible heresy, to say that seriousness is a vice. It is really a natural trend or lapse into taking one's self gravely, because it is the easiest thing to do. It is much easier to write a good* Times *leading article than a good joke in* Punch. *For solemnity flows out of men naturally; but laughter is a leap. It is easy to be heavy: hard to be light. Satan fell by force of gravity.*

His own, that is: Satan fell by force of his own gravity. By taking himself too seriously—by taking himself with ultimate seriousness—Satan fell. His weight became too much for him to bear, and so he fell. Crashed. Cratered. Isn't that rather like the modern gnostic mindset? Because nothing in the world counts, only *I* count: only my imperial autonomous self-generating *self* counts. Now *that's* heavy; far too heavy. A sacramental outlook on the world teaches us that, yes, we count (and infinitely). But so does everyone else. Moreover, everyone and everything are caught up in the same cosmic drama in which we find ourselves. That gives us some distance on us, which can lead to laughter, which is another window into the transcendent. Catholics laugh; gnostics frown.

---

### *On the Dangers in Narrow Worldliness*

*There is only one thing that can never go past a certain point in its dalliance with oppression—and that is orthodoxy. I may, it is true, twist orthodoxy so as partly to justify a tyrant. But I can easily make up a German philosophy to justify him entirely.*

Gnosticism is dangerous not only for your mental and spiritual health but also for your political health—as well as everyone else's. Take the more assertive scientists on the frontiers of today's biotech revolution. These men and women are highly sophisticated, supremely intelligent gnostics, for whom *nothing* is a given. And they'll tell you quite openly (if usually on the second or third drink, after hours at an academic conference) that they're in the immortality business: making human beings immortal, or as immortal as we want to be, until boredom or some other factor causes us to want to die of our own will. Humankind, in their view, is infinitely plastic; remanufacturable, if you will. And that's what they intend to do—remanufacture the human condition by manufacturing human beings.

Anyone who imagines that that can be done without massive coercion hasn't read Huxley. The brave new world—the gnostic world writ large—is a world of overwhelming coercion in the name of the highest ideals. The sacramental imagination is a barrier against the brave new world because it teaches us that the *givens* in this world have meaning—including the final givenness, which is death.

---

### *On God's Transcendence and Us*

> *By insisting specially on the immanence of God we get introspection, self-isolation, quietism, social indifference—Tibet. By insisting specially on the transcendence of God we get wonder, curiosity, moral and political adventure, righteous indignation—Christendom. Insisting that God is inside man, man is always inside himself. By insisting that God transcends man, man has transcended himself.*

The sacramental imagination builds civilizations. It's precisely *because* medieval Frenchmen believed in a world sacramentally configured—a world in which the true, good, and beautiful could be revealed through *stuff*—that they could build the great towers and fashion the miraculously luminous stained glass of Chartres (which we'll be visiting in due course). It's precisely because the late Frederick Hart had a sacramental imagination that he could sculpt such lifelike figures at the Vietnam Veterans Memorial—and such a magnificent evocation of the creation over the main doors of Washington Cathedral. If who we are and what we do *counts*, then it's worth being good, and it's worth doing as well as we can with what materials and talent we have at hand. If *nothing* counts—if the world is simply an ephemeral stage for working out the "needs" of my *self*—then why sculpt? Why paint? Why write poetry or compose music? Or, perhaps better, why do any of that in any way other than as a protest against the emptiness and meaninglessness of it all?

---

In a fine, book-length essay on St. Thomas Aquinas, G. K. Chesterton had this to say about his times, which have set the stage for yours: "As the eighteenth century thought itself the Age of Reason, and the nineteenth century thought itself the Age of Common Sense, the twentieth century cannot . . . think itself anything but the Age of Uncommon Nonsense." The uncommon nonsense that has spilled over from the twentieth century into the twenty-first is the gnostic nonsense that takes everything in the human condition as infinitely malleable and infinitely plastic. As GKC noted above, this strange attitude involves a deep disloyalty to the world, even as it imagines itself to be taking the world seriously by denying the transcendent.

Confronted by this disloyalty, Catholicism must declare its loyalty to the world—as created, redeemed, and sanctified by God, which is *the world as it is, transformed.* Declaring our loyalty to the world, Catholics propose a different reading of history. It's certainly possible to read "history" and learn something about the truth of history, according to the conventional chapter headings: Ancient Civilizations, Greece and Rome, The Middle Ages, Renaissance and Reformation, The Age of Revolution, The Age of Science, The Space Age. The sacramental imagination suggests another set of chapter headings: Creation, Fall, Promise, Prophecy, Incarnation, Redemption, Sanctification, The Kingdom.

The trick is to see, with Chesterton, that *the two stories are one story*. "World history" (as shown on the History Channel) and salvation history aren't running on parallel tracks. Salvation history *is* the human story, read in its true depth and against an appropriately ample horizon. Thus the romance of orthodoxy—getting the story of salvation history straight as *His*-story—*is* the romance of the world. And the adventure of orthodoxy is the greatest of *human* adventures. It's not an add-on, a kind of spiritual frequent flyer upgrade. It's the real deal, the thing itself. That's what the sacramental imagination teaches us.

The sacramental imagination gets the world into proper focus. Its critics often say that the Catholic Church is all about denying the world and ourselves; G. K. Chesterton insisted that Catholicism was about thick steaks, cigars, pubs, and laughter. Catholicism is more than that, of course. But it's also that, and to miss that is to miss something crucial in the Catholic world. The Catholic world isn't nervous about its legitimate pleasures. In fact, it's a world in which those pleasures can be fully enjoyed because they're understood for what they really are—anticipations of the joy that awaits us in the Kingdom of God.

And that, I suggest, is a lot more appealing than granola-and-Corona-Lite gnosticism.

But let's end this on a more literary than gustatory note. Chesterton's was a remarkably clean prose; as you've seen from the brief citations we've been pondering, his genius lay in giving unexpected twists to familiar things. Gerard Manley Hopkins was a different kind of literary man, whose genius involved sprung rhythms, word inventions, and a deliberate breaking of the conventions. As far as I know, Hopkins never frequented the Olde Cheshire Cheese. But it's entirely appropriate to finish our reflections here with a reading from this ascetic Jesuit.

What unites Chesterton and Hopkins is that both were saturated with the sacramental imagination. So let me end this letter, not with Hopkins's more familiar poem about the sacramentality of *stuff*, "God's Grandeur" ("The world is charged with the grandeur of God / It will flame out, like shining from shook foil . . . "), but with a less familiar hymn to the truth and beauty found in a profoundly Catholic loyalty to the world, to the open-ended givenness of things:

*Glory be to God for dappled things–*
*For skies of couple-colour as a brinded cow;*
*For rose-moles all in stipple upon trout that swim;*
*Fresh-firecoal chestnut-falls; finches' wings;*
*Landscape plotted and pieced—fold, fallow, and plough;*
*And all trades, their gear and tackle and trim.*

*All things counter, original, spare, strange;*
*Whatever is fickle, freckled (who knows how?)*
*With swift, slow; sweet, sour; adazzle, dim;*
*He fathers-forth whose beauty is past change:*
*Praise him.*

7

## Castle Howard, Yorkshire, England—*Brideshead Revisited* and the Ladder of Love

Castle Howard in Yorkshire has been home to descendants of the fourth duke of Norfolk for more than three hundred years. This masterpiece of architecture, decoration, and landscaping is set in a thousand-acre park, replete with rolling lawns, lakes, a magnificent rose garden, and a great fountain; the fountain's centerpiece is a Portland stone rendition of Atlas holding the earth on his shoulders. The main building, crowned by an ornate dome, borders three sides of a large landscaped courtyard. Going inside, you'll find Chippendale and Sheraton furniture, paintings by Gainsborough, Holbein, Joshua Reynolds, and Peter Paul Rubens, and statuary gathered from ancient Greece and Rome. Castle Howard got a lot of attention in the early 1980s when it was used in filming Evelyn Waugh's novel, *Brideshead Revisited*. And while it seems that this remarkable country estate was only one of several models for the fictional "Brideshead," home to the aristocratic Flyte family, that really doesn't matter. What counts is what happened in a place like this, in Evelyn Waugh's deeply Catholic imagination.

*Brideshead Revisited* is one of the few novels to be successfully "translated" into a film—in this case, a ten-hour British made-for-television extravaganza with an all-star cast: Jeremy Irons, Anthony Andrews, Diana Quick, Sir Laurence Olivier, Sir John Gielgud, Claire Bloom. I hope you'll read the book and then watch the film. When you do, I think you'll agree that Castle Howard/Brideshead is not simply the setting for much of the novel's action and the film's beauty. Through Waugh's artistry and insight, it becomes a kind of Everyplace in which we can watch the unfolding of a Catholic conversion—a privileged place where we can watch a man learning to climb the ladder of love.

Waugh himself found that ladder a steep one. Accosted at a party by a formidable matron who asked him how he, a prominent Catholic convert, could be so rude, Waugh replied, "Madame, were it not for the Faith, I should scarcely be human." Some might regard that as yet another example of Waugh's extraordinary eccentricity—the kind of anarchic humor that once led him to ask a superior officer in the Royal Marines whether it was true that "in the Romanian army no one beneath the rank of Major is permitted to use lipstick"? But I don't think so. For here is Waugh, in a more sober and reflective moment, writing essentially the same thing about the steepness of the ladder of love to his friend and fellow author, Edith Sitwell, when she was received into the Catholic Church:

> *Should I as Godfather warn you of probable shocks in the human aspect of Catholicism? Not all priests are as clever and kind as Father D'Arcy and Father Caraman. (The incident in my book of going to confession to a spy is a genuine experience.) But I am sure you know the world well enough to expect Catholic boors and prigs and crooks and cads. I always think to myself: "I know I am awful. But how much more awful I should be without the Faith." One of the joys of Catholic life is to recognize the little sparks of good everywhere, as well as the fire of the saints.*

One way to think about *Brideshead Revisited* and its insight into Catholicism is to think of it as a story in which those small sparks of goodness are slowly fanned into the flame of genuine conversion—despite some hard resistance from the principal characters.

---

It will do scant justice to the richness of Waugh's novel, but let me give you a desperately brief summary of the plot. The protagonist is Charles Ryder, a lonely, artistically inclined young man who has been sent to Oxford by his determinedly off-hand father, his mother having died years before. There Ryder meets and befriends Sebastian Flyte, youngest son of Lord Marchmain, hereditary master of Brideshead. Sebastian, who carries a Teddy bear named Aloysius, is at the center of an Oxonian circle of aesthetes and cranks. Yet even as he fritters away his Oxford days in four-hour lunches and drunken nocturnal escapades, Sebastian introduces Ryder to the wonders of natural beauty and the intensity of adolescent male friendship. As that friendship unfolds, Sebastian brings Ryder on several occasions to Brideshead itself. There Charles, overwhelmed by the sensuousness of the place, undergoes what he calls a "conversion to the baroque." The mystery of the Flyte family and its relationship to the Catholic Church intensifies when Sebastian, during summer break from university, takes Charles to meet his father, who lives in Venice with a wise and discerning mistress, having abandoned his wife and England after service in the First World War.

As Sebastian slowly sinks into alcoholism, Charles's friendship with Sebastian's beautiful sister, Julia, ripens—even as his relationship with the pious Lady Marchmain deteriorates. Stoically bearing her husband's infidelity and hatred, Lady Marchmain has remained at Brideshead, where she spends hours a day in the art nouveau chapel Lord Marchmain built her as a wedding present. Her intense but humanly inept piety has an element of the tragic about it, suggests her younger daughter, Cordelia: "When people wanted to hate God they hated Mummy." That turns out to be the case with Lord Marchmain himself, who returns to Brideshead after his wife's death. Charles Ryder, who has become a successful painter, and Julia are now living together at the great house after the failure of their marriages: Julia's to Rex Mottram, a soulless politician, and Ryder's to Celia Mulcaster, the society-conscious sister of a boorish Oxford classmate. After his brittle elder son, Bridey, marries a not altogether attractive widow, Lord Marchmain decides to leave Brideshead to

Julia, thumbing his nose at the proprieties and effectively disinheriting the son who most closely resembles the wife he abandoned.

As the hand of death tightens around Lord Marchmain's throat, a fierce argument breaks out between Charles and Julia. Bridey is determined to have a local priest called to Brideshead to see his dying father; Charles is just as determined that no such concession be made to what he and, he assumes, Lord Marchmain, regard as superstition. Julia, struggling with her own conscience and her lover's incomprehension, finally agrees to the visit when Lord Marchmain is on his deathbed, seemingly comatose. At the bedside, Charles finds himself torn:

> *Then I knelt, too, and prayed: "O God, if there is a God, forgive him his sins, if there is such a thing as sin . . ." I suddenly felt the longing for a sign, if only of courtesy, if only for the sake of the woman I loved, who knelt in front of me, praying, I knew, for a sign. It seemed so small a thing that was asked, the bare acknowledgment of a present, a nod in the crowd . . .*
>
> *The priest took the little silver box from his pocket and spoke again in Latin, touching the dying man with an oily wad; he finished what he had to do, put away the box, and gave the final blessing. Suddenly Lord Marchmain moved his hand to his forehead; I thought he had felt the touch of the chrism and was wiping it away. "O God," I prayed, "don't let him do that." But there was no need for fear; the hand moved slowly down his breast, then to his shoulder,*

> *and Lord Marchmain made the sign of the cross. Then I knew that the sign I had asked for was not a little thing, not a passing nod of recognition, and a phrase came back to me from my childhood of the veil of the temple being rent from top to bottom.*

Later that day, Charles and Julia meet by themselves and admit to each other what their hearts had sensed for some time. Something terrible and wondrous had been confirmed at Lord Marchmain's death—that, as Julia puts it, "I can't shut myself out from [God's] mercy . . . the bad thing I was on the point of doing, that I'm not quite bad enough to do [is] to set up a rival good to God's . . . Now we shall both be alone, and I shall have no way of making you understand." To which Charles replies, "I don't want to make it any easier for you . . . I hope your heart may break; but I do understand." Then they part.

Years later, Ryder, now a captain, returns to a Brideshead commandeered by the army as a training depot during World War II. He is a convert to Catholicism, newly struck by the significance, for his own life and those of the Flytes he loved, of the "small red flame" in the chapel he had once disdained aesthetically. And as this often saddened man leaves the chapel, his subaltern remarks, "You're looking unusually cheerful today."

---

Critics have often missed what seems to me the obvious, unmistakable thread running through *Brideshead Revisited.* Some, concentrating on the brilliant evocation of Oxford undergraduate life in the twenties, imagine it as another exercise in Waugh's social satire. In a Britain starved of luxuries during and after the Second World War, some read *Brideshead* as a nostalgic evocation of a more sumptuous past, even as others take the novel as further evidence for Waugh's snobbery. All of these readings quite miss the main point. The theme of *Brideshead Revisited* is exactly what Waugh said it was in his preface to the revised edition: "the operation of divine grace on a group of diverse but closely connected characters." This is a novel about conversion, and conversion understood as a climb up the sometimes steep steps of the ladder of love.

Seen another way, Charles Ryder is a man who grows from lesser affections to harder, yet truer loves. Evelyn Waugh's Catholic genius really kicks in, though, when we understand that Charles grows into the richest of loves—love for God in Christ—not merely *from* lesser loves but *through* them.

Starved of love as a boy by his cold, aloof father, he climbs one rung up the ladder of love through his friendship with Sebastian—even if that friendship involved a dalliance with what Ryder later describes as a "naughtiness . . . high in the catalogue of grave sins." But the love that Charles and Sebastian share is an immature one, as Ryder himself admits; Oxford and the house at Brideshead and Venice with Sebastian were "a brief spell of what I had never known, a happy childhood." Sebastian, fearing the loss of that happy childhood, escapes into alcoholism (and finally finds a home as a sometimes drunk, sometimes sober lay doorman at a North African monastery). Sebastian's own fear of adult love, and the responsibility it entails, doesn't destroy his friendship with Ryder but limits its scope and depth.

Ryder's love for Julia is higher and nobler than his love for Sebastian because it's a love directed to a truer end—even though it's an adulterous love on both sides. But this love, too, has it limits. It is also love-as-escape, the effort to create a new and solitary Arcadia with Julia at Brideshead, like the Arcadia that life at Oxford in the first flush of friendship with Sebastian had been. Yet even as they try to convince themselves that this is the genuine love for which they have been yearning, Julia seems ineffably and inexplicably sad; Bridey's characteristically tactless (if accurate) remark about her "living in sin" with Charles sends her into a rage of anger and tears. Similar outbursts follow, and Julia slowly begins to recognize that, while her anger seems aimed at her lover, its real target is herself. The deathbed drama of Lord Marchmain crystallizes in both Julia and Charles the realization that their love, however deep, cannot be a new Arcadia—there is no escape to any such mythical paradise from the truth about love and its demands. Recognizing that, Charles and Julia together take the next and even harder step up the ladder of love when, by mutual consent, they agree to part. Lesser loves have led to higher loves, and ultimately to a confrontation at Lord Marchmain's deathbed with the Love that is the hardest, most brilliant of all—the love of God, manifest in Christ, which shows us the truth about ourselves and our loving.

I learned a lot of this from my friend Douglas Lane Patey, who teaches at Smith College and strikes me as Waugh's most insightful literary interpreter. As Doug Patey once noted, Waugh intuitively understood the Catholic critique of modern sentimentality; he knew that love is not merely a feeling or sentiment, but rather a spiritual drive within us, a drive for communion, for "man is a being motivated by an inbuilt hunger for an adequate object of love." Thus Waugh takes Charles Ryder through a series of loves that form the stages of a spiritual ascent "from Sebastian through Julia to God. Each lesser love is real and valuable, but at the same time inadequate: each is a means pointing beyond itself to a more satisfactory end. And because the progression embodies a providential design, each is a seeming detour or retrogression than in fact constitutes an advance."

This deeply Catholic reading of the spiritual life may help explain why some critics regard *Brideshead* as little more than an evocative period piece—and why the back cover of a recent Penguin paperback edition of the book gets it spectacularly, smashingly wrong when it sums up Charles Ryder's journey as one in which he "finally comes to recognize his spiritual and social distance" from this "doomed Catholic family." Once again, Professor Patey is an able guide when he suggests that *Brideshead* is, rather, the story of "a providential plan: a design by which, in the usual manner of providence, good is educed from ill, meaning from the seeming chaos of events." Waugh, no fool, knew he was writing against the grain of modern sensibility by making divine providence the subtle engine of his story. Perhaps that's why, in a brilliant set piece, he puts the contemporary skeptic's view of Christianity in the mouth of a young, agnostic Charles Ryder, before Charles begins to feel the twitch of a divine pull on the thread of his own life. Thus Charles's description of himself during the early phase of his relationship with the Flyte family:

> *I had no religion. . . . The view implicit in my education was that the basic narrative of Christianity had long been exposed as a myth, and that opinion was now divided as to whether its ethical teaching was of present value, a division in which the main weight went against it; religion was a hobby which some people professed and others did not; at the best it was slightly ornamental, at the worst it was the province of "complexes" and "inhibitions"—catchwords of the decade—and of the intolerance, hypocrisy, and sheer stupidity attributed to it for centuries. No one had ever suggested to me that these quaint observances expressed a coherent philosophical system and intransigent historical claims; nor, had they done, would I have been much interested.*

Nor are some—perhaps many—"interested" today. And this brings into focus one of the great questions *Brideshead* puts squarely before you: Is life a permanent pleasure hunt, as so much of contemporary culture suggests (and as Charles Ryder once imagined)? Or is life a matter of learning-to-love? As I read it, *Brideshead Revisited* is a powerful invitation to invest in love. Which is, to be sure, a risky investment. But taking the risk of a genuine love, a love that attaches itself to what is truly worthy of the gift of one's self, is the only way to satisfy that yearning for communion that is at the heart of our humanity. Hard as love can be, love is the only eternal reality—for God himself is Love.

I'd be misleading you if I suggested that any of this is easy. It isn't, and Waugh knew it. That's why *Brideshead Revisited* doesn't smooth over the travail of climbing the ladder of love. During their idyllic Oxford days, Sebastian keeps telling Charles Ryder that he wishes it weren't true: "I suppose they try and make you believe an awful lot of nonsense," the skeptical Charles asks his friend about Catholicism. "Is it nonsense?" Sebastian replies, somberly. "I wish it were. It sometimes sounds terribly sensible to me."

A similar struggle with that challenging link between truth and love takes place in Ryder's relationship with Julia. On the night that Bridey announces his engagement, he also mentions that his intended, a "woman of strict Catholic principle fortified by the prejudices of the middle class," would never agree to being Charles and Julia's guest at Brideshead. "I couldn't possibly bring her here," Bridey continues. "It is a matter of indifference to me whether you choose to live in sin with Rex or Charles or both—I have always avoided inquiry into the details of your *ménage*—but in no case would Beryl consent to be your guest." After Julia storms out of the room in tears, she calms herself and she and Charles walk out on the lawn to the great Atlas fountain. Trying to distract Julia from Bridey's comment, Ryder asks, "You do know at heart that it's all bosh, don't you?" "How I wish it was!" Julia replies; and then Charles remembers—"Sebastian once said almost the same thing to me." But Charles still doesn't understand the ferment in Julia's soul. As they stand by the fountain, he tries another distracting conversational gambit: what they've been through that night, he suggests, is "like the setting of a comedy." Or perhaps it was "Drama. Tragedy.

Farce. What you will. This is the reconciliation scene." At which Julia explodes again: "Oh, don't talk in that damned bounderish way. Why must you see everything second-hand?" Although she's not yet ready to accept all its implications, Julia has begun to understand that the love for which she has been yearning can never be "second-hand," can never be a matter of acting a part. The only true comedy, she is beginning to intuit, is the divine comedy.

Charles's friendship with Sebastian, Doug Patey suggests, was "a kind of secular communion." His relationship with Julia takes place on a higher rung of the ladder of love, but it's still a spiritually deformed love, an incomplete communion—indeed, a communion that can never be complete, and thus must be abandoned, at least in its present form. Love, and the truth about a true love's true object, can never be separated. And that is why Charles, on the brink of conversion, can say, and mean without meanness, "I don't want to make it easier for you. I hope your heart may break. But I do understand."

---

Why is love so hard a thing to grow into? A contemporary of Waugh's, the great English apologist C. S. Lewis, was probably on to the beginning of an answer when he once observed that, for most of us as we now are, the joys of heaven would be an "acquired taste." Dante had the same idea—he had to become accustomed to heaven in his journey through the *Paradiso*; he had to learn to see things as they really are. That's why life cannot be lived secondhand, as Julia angrily tells Charles. Christians have to learn to live with reality, with the truth about truth and the truth about love, if we're going to fulfill our human and spiritual destiny and live happily forever with God—the God who is Truth and Love all the way through. That takes getting used to. And that's what the spiritual life is—climbing the ladder of love, with the help and prod of grace, to that summit where we can be happy living with Love itself, forever. For there, at the top of the ladder, we find the Love that is capable of fulfilling love's longing for an absolute fulfillment.

All over the London Underground—on the walls, tiled floors, and even London Underground souvenir T-shirts—riders are confronted with an admonition: "Mind the Gap." The designers of London's colossal subway system thought themselves offering a sensible warning about the danger of getting your foot caught between the edge of the train and the subway platform; in fact, they were giving us a metaphor and a motto for our growth in faith, hope, and love. We all live in the "gap" between the person we are today and the person we ought to be. That's the inherent *dramatic* structure of the spiritual life and the moral life. Living in and closing that gap—better: living in and letting God's grace, at work in our lives, close the gap—is a matter of becoming the kind of people who can live with God forever, the kind of people for whom heaven is a (super)natural pleasure, not an acquired taste.

Those people have learned, among other things, that sin and forgiveness are the warp and woof of the Christian life. Julia explodes at Bridey's crude comment about her "living in sin" precisely because she knows he's right. For Julia to grow into love, she has to accept that she's been living as she shouldn't, and that the only remedy for that is to stop, confess, and seek forgiveness and reconciliation. It's not enough to say "I take responsibility," the ubiquitous catchall for *not* taking real responsibility in our society. We have to take the consequences that go along with the responsibility, even if that means being pulled, yet again, up another steep rung on the ladder of love. In a society that isn't altogether secure in saying "This is right" and "This is wrong," period, "I take responsibility" is what irresponsible people often say to deflect attention from their irresponsibility—to change the subject, to get on with getting on. That's not the way Christians climb the ladder of love. That's not the way we become lovers who can live with Love for all eternity. That's not how our sundry human comedies (and tragedies) are integrated into the divine comedy—"the love that moves the sun and the other stars," as Dante ended the greatest poem ever.

---

*Brideshead Revisited*, the film, has a marvelous soundtrack composed by Geoffrey Burgon. Its elegiac main theme, whether rendered by flute, French horn, or a single muted trumpet, reminds us that love, while no easy business, *is* at the center of our humanity—and the *Brideshead* theme does that without descending into sentimentality. So does one of the great hymns of the Catholic tradition, *Ubi caritas et amor*, typically sung at the Mass of the Lord's Supper on Holy Thursday while the priest washes the feet of a dozen congregants (as Jesus washed his disciples feet on their last night together), or during the congregation's procession to holy communion. The text is a simple one:

*Ubi caritas et amor, Deus ibi est.*
*Congregavit nos in unum Christi amor.*
*Exultemus, et in ipso iucundemur.*
*Timeamus, et amemus Deum vivum,*
*et ex corde diligamus nos sincero.*

*Where charity and love are, there God is.*
*We have been brought together as one in the love*
*of Christ.*
*Let us exult and rejoice in him.*
*May we fear and love the living God,*
*and may we love with a sincere heart.*

Take a moment now and listen to the setting of this ancient text by the modern French composer Maurice Duruflé, who died in 1986; it's the first of his *Four Motets*, opus 10. Faithful to the hymn's foundations in Gregorian chant, Duruflé marries this melodic line to a contemporary four-part harmony in which sopranos and altos, tenors and basses, remind each other, back and forth, that *ubi caritas et amor, Deus ibi est.* The entire motet lasts less than two minutes but captures, through some mysterious interplay of text and musical setting, everything we've been exploring here: the human thirst for love, the struggle to find appropriate loves, the ladder of love to which Christ beckons us, the forgiveness of Christ that makes the ascent to truer loves possible, becoming the kind of lover who can love Love forever. I have often thought that I should like to listen to certain pieces of music on my deathbed (if God is kind enough to grant me a deathbed); Duruflé's *Ubi caritas* would certainly be one of them.

For here we really are at the center of the Catholic and Christian claim—that love is the most living thing there is, for God himself is love. *This* is "the love that moves the sun and the other stars." This is what makes us, and this is what we are made for—we are made for love, so that we may live with Love.

There's another historic site in England where the bracing demands of love come into focus—the Tower of London, in the cell in which St. Thomas More lived for the last fifteen months of his life. You know his story from another great film, *A Man for All Seasons*. You may remember the heart-wrenching scene in the final act, when More's family is allowed into that cell to talk him into truckling to the king's determination to make himself head of the Church in England. More's beloved daughter Margaret, whom he has taken care to educate in the classics, is designated to appeal to both her father's heart and mind:

More: *You want me to swear to the Act of Succession?*

Margaret: *"God more regards the thoughts of the heart than the words of the mouth." Or so you've always told me.*

More: *Yes.*

Margaret: *Then say the words of the oath and in your heart think otherwise.*

More: *What is an oath but words we say to God?*

Margaret: *That's very neat.*

More: *Do you mean it isn't true?*

Margaret: *No, it's true.*

More: *Then it's a poor argument to call it "neat," Meg. When a man takes an oath, Meg, he's holding his whole self in his own hands. Like water. And if he opens his fingers then—he needn't hope to find himself again. Some men aren't capable of this, but I'd be loathe to think your father one of them.*

Margaret tries another tack, arguing that More is making himself into a hero. He parries that thrust easily enough—with the world being what it is, "why then perhaps we *must* stand fast a little, even at the risk of being heroes." Margaret, close to tears, then cries out: "But in reason! Haven't you done as much as God can reasonably want?" To which More replies, haltingly, "Well . . . finally . . . it isn't a matter of reason; finally it's a matter of love."

Love of what? Of truth, I suggest—the truth with which Christ seizes our lives. And what is that truth? It is the truth that we have come from love, that we have been redeemed by an infinite love, and that we are destined for an eternity of love with Love itself. In the final analysis, this isn't something that's settled by rationality, by argument. It's settled, in an often unsettling way, by Someone. It's a matter of being seized by the Truth who is Love—the Love that became incarnate in the world in Jesus of Nazareth, especially in his suffering, death, and resurrection.

To be seized by the truth mirrored in the face of Christ, and to love that truth with everything we have in us, is emphatically not something we do by ourselves. We meet Christ in his Church, which Catholicism often calls the "mystical body of Christ." The Church, as you well know, is a very earthen vessel, full of cracks and fissures. Learning about that can also be a step up the ladder of love; let me give you an example.

When I was a boy, our parish pastor was a kind of godlike figure to me. A "late vocation," he had been a Princeton classmate of F. Scott Fitzgerald, had made money on Wall Street, and seemed to know everyone worth knowing. He'd been close to my paternal grandparents and was a frequent guest in our home. When, during high school, I discovered that he was an alcoholic I was devastated. That devastation turned, I must confess, to the feelings of contempt that come from learning abruptly about an idol's clay feet, especially during those adolescent years with their painful combination of certainties and uncertainties.

I rarely saw this man in my twenties. But in 1987, I was returning to my old parish to lecture on my first major book, and I somehow got it into my head that I should visit him at the retirement home where he was then living—or, more precisely, dying of throat cancer. His condition made it difficult to talk, but we managed a fifteen-minute conversation and I gave him a copy of the book, assuming that he was too ill to come to my lecture. When I was taking my leave, he asked me to come closer. Reaching up from his wheelchair to draw me into a half embrace, he whispered, in his cancer-hoarsened voice, "You know that I have always loved your family." I couldn't hold back the tears and told him that now I knew. That night, he staggered on a cane into the back of the parish hall; he had taken a cab from his retirement home and he could only stay for five minutes. But he was going to give witness, if only for that long, to the fact that he had loved me, and loved my family.

I don't mean to be overly dramatic, but that afternoon and evening were a great lesson for me in the absolute centrality of love within Catholicism. Was my old pastor a weak, sinful man? Yes, and I had to come to grips with that. Was he also a man who, in the final analysis, had given his life to love, and to Love? That's how he taught me to read his life during that last time we were together. The giving, and the loving, had been transformed by Love itself into what St. Paul calls in Philippians 4:18 an "acceptable sacrifice": a sacrifice in which all that he had done wrong had been consumed by fire.

His ladder of love had been a steep one; indeed, he'd fallen off it more than once. I thank God that he lived long enough, and that Providence brought us back together again, so that I could learn how, through the falls, he had completed the climb—and so I could learn one last lesson from him.

---

What does all this business about love and Love come down to for you? Simply this: never settle for less than the spiritual and moral grandeur which, by grace, can be yours. They are your baptismal birthright as a Christian.

You will fail. You will stumble on the ladder of love, and you will fall. That's no reason to lower the bar of expectation. That's a reason to get up, dust yourself off, seek forgiveness and reconciliation, and try again. If you settle for anything less than the greatness for which you were made—the greatness that became your destiny at baptism—you're cheating yourself. If you settle for anything less than the greatness that has been made possible for you by Christ, you're ignoring the twitch of the divine weaver on the thread of your life. Let His grace lift you up to where, in your heart of hearts, you want to be.

# 8

## The Sistine Chapel, Rome—Body Language, God Talk, and the Visible Invisible

The Sistine Chapel in Rome may well be the most extraordinary room in the world. Millions of people come here every year to admire the beauty of the chapel's decoration: the ceiling frescoes and *Last Judgment* of Michelangelo; the scenes from the life of Christ and the life of Moses that rim the chapel walls, painted by such masters as Botticelli, Ghirlandaio, Perugino, Pinturicchio, and Signorelli. It's usually a very busy place.

Even if you come here during the height of the tourist season, you may notice a curiosity—when tourists enter the Sistine Chapel, the buzz that usually surrounds tour groups often fades away, if only briefly. People are stunned into silence, or at least something approaching silence. Is that a reaction to the magnificence of the frescoes' colors, which, since their restoration, are far bolder than any photograph can convey?

Are visitors awestruck at the human genius that could produce such painting? I suspect the answer is yes to both.

But let me suggest that something else—something *more*—is going on here. A great travel writer, H. V. Morton, once said that "a visit to Rome is not a matter of discovery, but of remembrance." That's what the Sistine Chapel does to visitors: it touches deeply rooted (and sometimes deeply buried) cultural and spiritual memories and intuitions. People are awestruck in the Sistine Chapel because, through the frescoes and what they arouse deep within us, this has become another borderland between the human and the divine.

Viewed one by one, in a picture book, Michelangelo's frescoes can seem overwhelming, even frightening, in their sheer physicality. Yet here in the Sistine Chapel, this painted architecture in which luminous, brilliant color is married to grand and inspiring form has an evocativeness and spiritual transparency about it. No matter what their religious disposition (or lack thereof), those who visit the Sistine Chapel can't help sensing that its beauty is a kind of window into the truth about the human—and about the yearning for the transcendent that is built into us.

That instinct is right. And that's because this shrine to the beauty of the human body is a privileged place of encounter with the beauty of God. The two go together.

---

The story of the Sistine Chapel is filled with controversy—not unlike a lot of Catholic history. It began, in 1475, as a combination papal chapel and fortification (as those surprising crenellations on the exterior suggest).

It's called the "Sistine" Chapel in honor of its builder, Pope Sixtus IV, a Franciscan member of the della Rovere clan, who sat on Peter's Chair from 1471 to 1484. There's nothing very complicated about the building itself—a rectangular space, 132 feet long, 44 feet wide, and 68 feet high: the dimensions of Solomon's temple. The hall is surmounted by a barrel vault; the ceiling is somewhat flattened by lateral vaulting; there are four sail-shaped pendentives in the corners of the ceiling. Twelve windows, six per side, provide natural light. The floor (too often overlooked) is a fine example of polychrome inlaid marble in the classic Roman Cosmati tradition. About two-thirds of the way down from the altar wall, a marble and iron *transenna*, a kind of rood screen, separates what would have been the congregation's space from the larger space reserved for the papal chapel—the pope, his cardinals, and sundry prelates of lesser rank.

Sixtus IV had the ceiling painted as a blue sky with golden stars. In fact, Sixtus seems to have been far less concerned about the ceiling (whose topography made it a real challenge for painters) than with the walls, for which he commissioned two biblical fresco cycles, the life of Moses on the south wall and the life of Christ on the north; as already noted, these splendid paintings were done by some of the great Renaissance masters (and are currently being restored). The choice of subject matter was deliberate. Sixtus evidently wanted to show, pictorially, the close connection between God's revelation of himself to the people of Israel and God's self-revelation in Christ.

In 1503, the cardinals chose another della Rovere pope, Sixtus's nephew Giuliano, who took the papal name Julius II. Shortly after his election, Julius had to deal with a structural crisis in his uncle's chapel. Cracks in the vault began to appear in 1504. And as if that weren't enough, the soft soil beneath the chapel was beginning to shift, the south wall had begun to tilt outward, and the whole ceiling was in danger of being pulled to pieces. Iron bars were installed in the ceiling masonry and the floor to hold the vault together and steady the foundation. By the end of 1504, the chapel had been stabilized, but the ceiling was a mess.

Julius wanted to commission the brilliant Florentine, Michelangelo, to replace the starry sky motif on the Sistine Chapel ceiling; he had already hired Michelangelo to sculpt him a colossal tomb. The great Bramante, who served Julius as papal architect, objected, perhaps for political and personal as well as professional reasons. Whatever his motives, Bramante was right in noting that Michelangelo had no experience in the extremely difficult maneuver the Italians called *di sotto in sù* (from below, upward)—frescoing on a high, curved ceiling so that those standing below imagine the painted figures to be suspended above them, floating in the air. Julius overruled Bramante. The real problem was that Michelangelo didn't want the commission and refused the pope, holing up in Florence. Julius II, however, was not a man to take no for an answer; after cajoling by various intermediaries failed, he simply ordered Michelangelo to return to Rome and submit. Not wanting to risk the papal wrath any further, the stubborn Florentine finally agreed.

Julius's original plan called for the ceiling to be covered with elaborate geometric designs, complemented by portraits of the twelve apostles in the triangular spandrels above the windows. Michelangelo toyed with bringing Julius's design alive, but he wasn't satisfied with it—not least because he wanted to do large-scale frescoes of the human body. Blunt as ever, Michelangelo informed Julius that the pope's design was *una cosa povera*—a poor thing. For some reason, Julius, who had a very short fuse, didn't explode but told Michelangelo to make a fresh design.

It was a monumental task. How was Michelangelo to cover 12,000 square feet of vaulted space with fresco on a surface that combined flat and curved space, large expanses and small corners, and make the entire design hang together? Michelangelo, who dreamed no small dreams, finally decided to create a visual epic of the human drama: the creation of the world and the early history of the human race would march across the vault from west to east in nine epic paintings (three on the creation of nature, three on the creation of humankind, three on the Noah story); ancient prophets and sibyls, heralds of humanity's redemption, would fill the spandrels; and crucial moments in the history of Israel would decorate the pendentives. It took four years to execute. When Rome saw it, on All Saints' Day, 1512, everyone from Julius II on down was stunned. Nothing like this had ever been seen before; nothing this magnificent had ever been done before.

Michelangelo, who always insisted that he was a sculptor rather than a painter, may have thought that he was finished with the Sistine Chapel when Julius finally stopped asking about the ceiling, "When will you be done?" Paul III, the fourth pope to succeed Julius II, had other ideas, however. In 1535 he asked the Florentine to execute a vast fresco of the Last Judgment on the chapel's altar wall, replacing several Perugino frescoes and two of the lunettes that Michelangelo himself had painted in 1512. This time, Michelangelo didn't resist. When the work was completed in 1541, all

Rome was, once again, awestruck—and some prudes were angry.

The *Last Judgment* is a massive swirl of imagery, centered on the triumphant figure of the Risen Christ, at once majestic and terrible, decisive and calm. Angels surround the Lord, carrying the instruments of his passion—the cross, the crown of thorns, the pillar of the scourging. At the bottom left, those who will be saved awake and are drawn up by the angels to the glory of heaven; on the right, the damned fall into hell, as Charon, the boatman of the Styx, wields his oar above their fleeing figures. The Virgin Mary is seated at her son's right, her face turned toward the saints. The apostles and martyrs carry the emblems of their suffering; in the folds of St. Bartholomew's flayed skin, Michelangelo painted a self-portrait. (The Florentine wasn't above settling scores through his work, either. The figure of Minos, the master of hell who appears at the bottom right with a snake encircling his torso, bears a not accidental similarity to Biagio da Cesena, the papal master of ceremonies. When da Cesena complained to Paul III, the pontiff replied that even he lacked the power to get someone out of hell.)

A Vatican guidebook somewhat primly notes that, while the unveiling of the *Last Judgment* aroused "stupor and admiration," it also resulted in "severe and malicious criticism, which has left its mark." It seems that prudes in Counter-Reformation Rome objected to the nudes in the *Last Judgment*. Consequently, about forty *braghe* (loincloths) were added to the painting, beginning in the late sixteenth century. But that was hardly the end of Sistine Chapel controversy.

By the mid–1960s, the Sistine Chapel was badly in need of restoration. Centuries of smoke, dust, bird droppings (the windows were often left open), the effects of candles and incense, and earlier inept efforts at fresco cleaning had taken their toll; the ceiling leaked, causing more damage to the paintings. So the roof was fixed and several of the wall frescoes were cleaned between 1964 and 1974. The real brawl began, however, with the proposal to clean Michelangelo's ceiling frescoes and *Last Judgment*. Several forests were sacrificed to provide the paper on which this controversy played itself out over a quarter century. Although some of the argument involved prudent concerns about the cleaning method and its long-term effects on the frescoes, other art historians and critics couldn't come to grips with the fact that the dark shadows they had attributed to the repressed Freudian crevices of Michelangelo's mind, or whatever, were in fact pigeon guano and lampblack.

Today, the restoration is almost universally considered a tremendous accomplishment. It took nine years to clean the ceiling a few inches at a time; another four years were required to clean the *Last Judgment*. In both instances, colors that hadn't been seen for centuries have been gloriously restored. What had once seemed a dark and somewhat forbidding space is now luminously bright. (John Paul II, who authorized the restoration, also had about half the loincloths removed from the *Last Judgment*, leaving the rest in place for historical purposes.)

Stand here, imagine the genius that produced the biblical stories and the genius that brought those stories alive in fresco—and then try to convince yourself that human beings are congealed stardust, an accident of evolutionary biology. Here, in this borderland where we can touch and sense the human heart's ardent desire to see God, the burden of proof is on the agnostic and the atheist. And here, too, the old canard that Catholicism deprecates the material, the physical, and the sexual is revealed for what it is—a lie.

---

On April 8, 1994, which happened to be Easter Friday, Pope John Paul II celebrated a Mass in the Sistine Chapel to mark the completion of the restoration of the Michelangelo frescoes. That Mass was the occasion for one of the most remarkable homilies of a remarkably eloquent pontificate. Pushing hard against the outside of the theological envelope, the Pope proposed that Michelangelo's frescoes were a kind of sacrament—a throbbingly visible reality through which we encounter the mystery of the invisible God. These works of "unparalleled beauty" evoked from those who saw them a passion to "profess our faith in God, Creator of all things seen and unseen," and to proclaim once again our faith in "Christ, King of the Ages, whose kingdom will have no end."

Despite the fact that they were painted decades apart, Michelangelo's two Sistine efforts had a deep theological relationship to one another, the Pope suggested: the *Last Judgment* in fact completes the proto-history of humankind on the ceiling. The beauties depicted in the first six frescos of the creation cycle—God bringing creation out of chaos, God creating the human world in Adam and Eve—give way to the three paintings of the story of Noah, with its reminder that human beings tend always to make a mess of the gift of the created world. But Noah's betrayal by his sons in his drunkenness (last of the ceiling's Genesis frescoes and a symbol of enduring human wickedness) isn't the end of the story. The creation story and the Noah story spill over, on the altar wall, into the story of redemption, synthesized in Michelangelo's stunning portrayal of the Last Judgment.

The *Last Judgment* is the "end" of the story in a deeper-than-chronological sense: the Christ who establishes his Kingdom and brings the righteous into it to reign with him forever thereby brings creation to its "end," in the sense of its purpose and its fulfillment. Life is not random and aimless, these glorious frescoes tell us. *There is purpose in the world, divine purpose*. In the Risen Christ, returned to judge history and the men and women of history, God brings to completion what he began at the far end of the chapel, by dividing light from darkness in the first moment of creation.

This Christ of the Last Judgment, the Pope continued, is "an extraordinary Christ . . . endowed with an ancient beauty." And that beauty is deeply enmeshed with "the glory of Christ's humanity," for the humanity of Jesus, born of the flesh and blood of Mary, was the vehicle by which God entered the world to set matters aright. Here, the Pope said, we come face-to-face with the Christ who "expresses in himself the whole mystery of the visibility of the Invisible."

Michelangelo, John Paul suggested, was a man of great Christian conviction and even greater artistic audacity. In his ceiling frescos, he had the courage to "admire with his own eyes" God at the very moment of creation, and especially in the creation of man. For Adam, made "in the image and likeness" of God (Genesis 1:26) is a "visible icon" of the Creator himself—and Adam is that icon precisely in his naked physical beauty. But Michelangelo didn't stop here. "With great daring," the Pope continued, the Florentine "even transferred this visible and corporal beauty to the Creator himself"—a bold move that stands just this side of blasphemy. Michelangelo knew where the boundary line was, though; he has taken us as far as pictorial art can go in representing "God clad in infinite majesty." Then he went no farther, for "everything which could be expressed has been expressed here." Although they must never be confused, the two realities with which Michelangelo's genius wrestled are nevertheless intimately connected: the human body is an icon of God's outpouring of himself to his creation; God himself is the "source of the integral beauty of the body."

In short, John Paul concluded, the Sistine Chapel is the "sanctuary of the theology of the human body." The beauty of man, male and female, created by God for an eternity of communion with the Creator, is completed in the beauty of the Risen Christ, come in glory to judge the living and the dead. Human bodies aren't objects. Human bodies are icons.

---

Some people, however, just don't get it.

The *New York Times* correspondent who covered that April 1994 rededication Mass was surprised that, preaching before Michelangelo's undraped nudes, John Paul "seemed not the least embarrassed, despite his frequent affirmations of the Church's conservative teachings on sex." Or perhaps that's what the editors in New York wrote into the reporter's copy. In any event, the *Times* had it exactly backward.

The Pope didn't celebrate Michelangelo's work as a "testimony to the beauty of man" *despite* the Catholic Church's teaching about sex but *because* of that teaching.

In a move that takes the argument about the sexual revolution as far beyond prudishness as you can imagine, John Paul has proposed that sexual love within the bond of faithful and fruitful marriage is nothing less than an icon of the interior life of God himself. That's right: the Catholic Church teaches that sex, as an expression of marital love and commitment, is another *sacramental* reality on the border between the ordinary and the extraordinary. Which is another way of saying that sex, rightly understood, helps teach us about God, even as it teaches us about ourselves.

Many young Catholics today are fascinated by John Paul II's "theology of the body," which he laid out in 129 general audience addresses between 1979 and 1984. Those highly compact addresses, dense with biblical, philosophical, literary, and theological analysis, can be a little daunting. Let me give you the briefest outline of the Pope's proposal.

John Paul begins with Genesis, which teaches that our bodies aren't just machines we live in. We *are* embodied, and the body through which I speak, write, play, love, and work is intrinsic to *me*. Remember what I wrote you before about the "gnostic imagination" and its deprecation of the physical? Here's the Catholic counterbid at its sharpest.

But how are we made, body and spirit, in the "image and likeness" of God, as Genesis describes us? Not only, the Pope suggests, in our capacity to think and choose, but also in *our capacity to live in communion with others—to make a gift of ourselves to others, as our lives are a gift to us*. That means that the "creation of man" wasn't finished until the creation of Eve, for only when there is Eve does Adam discover that the loneliness of the human condition can be overcome in that mysterious process by which we give ourselves to another—and find that we've been enriched by doing so. Love, the creation stories tell us, is not a zero-sum game; neither is life. The only way to find ourselves is to give ourselves away. This *Law of the Gift* is the deep imprint of the "image of God" in us, for that is what God is in himself: God the Holy Trinity—Father, Son, and Holy Spirit—is a communion of self-giving love, received and returned for all eternity.

So what happened? Why did Adam and Eve start to feel ashamed of their nakedness? When Adam and Eve lived their freedom as a free gift of self, they felt no shame; when they began using each other, they felt shame. The "original sin," John Paul suggests, is the perennial human tendency to ignore the Law of the Gift, the law of self-giving that was built into us "in the beginning," as the first verse of the Bible puts it. Adam and Eve "sinned," not because God peremptorily decreed that "x = sin," but because they failed to live the truth built into them. As do we all. So the Adam and Eve stories in Genesis teach a fundamental moral and spiritual lesson about our lives and our loves: *human happiness depends on self-giving, not self-assertion*.

The second part of the "theology of the body" takes up a New Testament text that has puzzled readers for centuries: Jesus' saying in the Sermon on the Mount that "everyone who looks at a woman lustfully has already committed adultery with her in his heart" (Matthew 5:27–28). Isn't that an impossibly, indeed insanely, high standard (and for everyone, women as well as men, for the temptation to lust isn't for men only)? On the contrary—John Paul suggests that this puzzling text is in fact a key to understanding our sexuality in a thoroughly humanistic way.

Remember that "original sin" is a corruption of something good: self-giving gets corrupted when it becomes self-assertion. That's what lust does. Lust and desire are two different things. If I'm truly attracted to someone, I want to make a gift of myself to that person for *his* good or *her* good, not just *my* good. Lust is the opposite of that self-giving; lust is the itch for transitory pleasure through the *use* of someone else, even the abuse of someone else. If a man looks lustfully rather than longingly at a woman, or a woman at a man, the "other" isn't a person any longer; the "other" is an object, an object for selfish gratification. There's no giving or receiving or mutual communion there.

The Catholic sexual ethic, John Paul proposes, redeems sexual love from the quicksand of lust. The usual charge is that Catholicism is nervous, even paranoid, about the erotic. The truth of the matter is that *the Catholic sexual ethic liberates the erotic by transforming longing into self-giving*, which leads to the kind of relationships that affirm the human dignity of both partners. Does Catholicism blunt desire? On the contrary, *the Catholic sexual ethic channels our desires "from the heart," so that desire leads to a true communion of persons, a true giving-and-receiving*. Which, to go back to a point made by the Pope, is how sexual love is an image of God in himself and an image of God's relationship to the world.

Catholicism isn't about "self-control," which is a psychological category. The Catholic sexual ethic is a matter of growing into *self-mastery*, which is a spiritual and moral category: the mastery of desire that lets us give ourselves to others intimately in a way that affirms the "other" in his or her giving and receiving. That's what Jesus means in the Beatitudes by "purity of heart."

Living and loving that way leads to holiness as well as satisfaction; it's a way to sanctify the world.

The third part of the "theology of the body" draws these themes together and teaches us that *marriage is one of those sacramental realities that takes us into the extraordinary that lies just on the far side of the ordinary*. Marriage is an icon of God's creation of the world, which was an act of divine love and self-outpouring. Marriage is also an icon of God's redemption of the world; as St. Paul teaches in Ephesians, the love of Christ for the Church is like the love of husband and wife. That creative and redeeming love isn't simply affection, important as affection is. Married love, the Pope suggests, is the human reality that best images the commitment, the intensity, indeed the *passion* of Christ's love for the Church, for which he laid down his life. And that is why John Paul can teach that sexual love within the bond of marriage can be an act of worship.

---

At which point you may be saying: this is just too much. But is it? The Church knows that sexual love within marriage isn't always ecstatic; but on a Catholic view of things, ecstasy is what love should aim for. Why? Because a thirst for the ecstatic is built into us—which is another way of saying that the thirst for God is built into us. That's what people sense in the Sistine Chapel. The beauty of the body, mirroring the beauty of God, awakens in us that latent thirst for ecstasy which is our thirst for communion with others and with God. Don't ever deny that thirst for the ecstatic. Don't be afraid of it.

And don't think you can satisfy that thirst by treating sex as another contact sport, which is what the sexual revolution has come down to. That's cheating yourself. Sex-as-contact-sport isn't any different from animal sexuality: impersonal, instinctive, a matter of "need." You're made for something far nobler and far more satisfying than that. You've been made for love, for a love freely offered and freely received, a love that includes permanent commitment. That's why, with John Paul II, we can call chastity the "integrity of love." Chastity isn't a laundry list of thou shalt not's. Chastity is the virtue by which I can love another *as a person*. And that's why *chaste* sexual love—the adjective makes perfect sense here—is *ecstatic* sexual love, in the original meaning of ecstasy: being "transported outside oneself." True sexual love is a matter of putting my emotional center in the care of another. You can make that kind of gift and you can receive a similar gift, because you're free: *your freedom is your capacity to make a free gift of yourself to others*. That's true of all friendship; it's particularly true of the special form of friendship that is marriage, which is sealed with, and expresses itself through, the blessing of sexual love.

And that brings us to another lesson to be teased out of the Sistine Chapel and the "theology of the body" it enshrines: *the Catholic context for thinking about sex is freedom, not prohibition*. Loving, not using—that's the deeply humane challenge the Catholic Church poses to the sexual revolution.

---

Perhaps some of the issues of sexual morality can be brought into clearer focus now. Confronting the tangles and confusions and passions of our sexuality, the first question a serious Catholic asks is *not*, What am I forbidden to do? The first *Catholic* question is, How do I express my sexuality in a way that affirms my human dignity? And there's no way to affirm *my* dignity without at the same time affirming the dignity of the "other." That's the context: *dignity*. Within that context, there are certain things we don't do, the Church teaches, and we don't do those things because they wound our dignity and corrupt the rhythm of giving-and-receiving that makes for a true communion between human beings.

When we confuse loving with self-pleasuring, our capacity to give ourselves to others atrophies; it can die. This is especially true when sexual solipsism is linked to pornography, which is about as clear an example there is of reducing the "other" to an object for my self-gratification. There's no growth in love in the illusory world of pornographic self-indulgence.

Why does premarital sex violate the integrity of love? Because, as my friend the Lutheran moral theologian Gilbert Meilaender once put it quite neatly, Christians only make love to people to whom they've made promises. Serious promise making, which is implied by the complete gift of self that sexual love embodies, isn't transitory, and it isn't serial.

Then, within the bond of marriage, there's the question of contraception. You've been bludgeoned, I'm sure, with the claim that Catholicism insists on an ideology of fertility at all costs. That, too, is a lie. The Catholic Church teaches that family planning is a moral responsibility. *The Catholic question is not whether a couple should plan their family, but how they should live that plan*. How do we best regulate fertility and live parenthood responsibly, while safeguarding the dignity of marriage (and especially of women) and honoring the spiritual and moral truth of married love as giving-and-receiving? The Church proposes that using the natural rhythms of biology to regulate fertility is a more humanistic way of living procreative responsibility than using chemical or mechanical contraceptives. In a culture in which "natural" has become one of secular society's sacred incantations, that teaching deserves something better than ridicule; it deserves to be engaged thoughtfully, as does the experience of tens of thousands of couples who have found their marriages enriched by natural family planning.

Then there is homosexuality. The gay movement is perhaps the most potent example of what I've been calling the "gnostic imagination" in our culture today. And that perhaps explains why Catholic Church is a principal target of gay activists. But at least let's get clear on what the debate is about. The Catholic Church teaches that homosexual acts are morally wrong because they cannot embody the complementarity, the rhythm of giving-and-receiving, built into our embodiedness as male and female, and because such acts are intrinsically incapable of generating life. The Church does *not* teach that a homosexual orientation is sinful; it does teach that homosexual desire is a disordered affection, a sign of spiritual disturbance.

Is this "prejudice," as gay activists charge? I don't think so. The Catholic Church flatly rejects the claim—which really is prejudice—that homosexually inclined persons are somehow subhuman. What the Church also teaches is that those homosexually inclined persons are called, *like everyone else*, to live the Law of the Gift built into us "from the beginning." When a brilliant young Catholic political commentator like Andrew Sullivan writes that his gay passions are "the very core of my being," the Church says, "No, that can't be right. Your desires can't be all you are; your own talent and political courage and insight testify against that. Give chastity a chance—a chance to remind you what really makes you . . . you."

No one suggests that any of this is easy, for homosexually inclined people or anyone else, in today's sex-saturated society. That's why the same Cardinal John O'Connor (the late archbishop of New York), who was frequently attacked by gay activists (who called him, among other things, a "fat cannibal" and a "creep in black skirts") would regularly visit Church-run hospices to comfort, talk with, and change the bedpans of AIDS patients. It wasn't an act; it wasn't PR. Cardinal O'Connor did this out of conviction—the same conviction that led him to teach the truth of Catholic faith, even when his critics called his cathedral that "house of walking swastikas on Fifth Avenue."

I think the cardinal's combination of tenacity and humility was a lesson for all of us. The Catholic Church teaches what it believes to be the truth given it by Christ—a truth whose most basic elements were first inscribed on the human heart "in the beginning." At the same time, the Church lives in solidarity with those very fallible human beings—all of us—who, in matters of chastity as well as in just about everything else, fall and struggle to get back up on our feet.

Jesus did that three times on the way to Calvary, according to the Stations of the Cross. We shouldn't expect anything different.

# 9

# St. Mary's Church, Greenville, South Carolina—Why and How We Pray

There are many kinds of "sublime" and many kinds of "transcendent" in the Catholic world. The Sistine Chapel is one obvious example of both. So is a rather different place—St. Mary's Church in Greenville, South Carolina. It doesn't have Perugino or Michelangelo frescoes. Popes haven't been elected there. But you don't need all that to experience the divine touching the mundane in the Catholic world. St. Mary's, Greenville, is as good a place as there is in North America to experience what Catholic worship is and ought to be—and then to think about why and how we pray, as a community and as individuals.

Catholics had been migrating to the Piedmont region of South Carolina since the first days of the American Republic, but it wasn't until 1872 that a resident pastor settled at Greenville. Missions had been conducted in the surrounding area for the previous twenty years, so St. Mary's Parish is reckoned to have been founded in

1852. The first parish church was consecrated in 1876 and dedicated to Our Lady of the Sacred Heart of Jesus, a new Marian devotion that originated in France in 1854. The church building you see here today was the work of two pastors, Monsignor Andrew Keene Gwynn and Monsignor Charles J. Baum, who, between them, ran St. Mary's for seventy-three years. At its sesquicentennial in 2002, St. Mary's parish included some two thousand families from a host of racial, ethnic, and economic backgrounds and circumstances, and its school educated 350 youngsters.

When the people of St. Mary's came to church on Sunday morning, July 1, 2001, they noticed that things had changed in the previous twenty-four hours. The tabernacle, which had been banished to the side of the sanctuary in 1984, had been restored to its proper place at the end of the long axis of the church, enthroned on the reredos at the rear of the sanctuary. A large icon of Mary had been hung—the first image of the parish patroness to be visible in the church for twenty years. Burlap banners made by second graders had been removed. The tattered paperback "worship resources" (which is what some confused people call "hymnals") had been removed from the pews and consigned to the parish dumpster; a music program for that Sunday's Mass had been made for every congregant. But these changes were merely a harbinger of what was coming next. It's safe to say that, in a century and a half, the people of St. Mary's had never heard an inaugural sermon like the one they heard from their new pastor, Father Jay Scott Newman, on the first Sunday of July 2001:

*I am Jay Scott Newman, and I am a disciple of the Lord Jesus Christ. I am also, by the grace of God, a priest of the New Covenant in the presbyteral order. And by the appointment of Robert, twelfth bishop of Charleston, I am now the sixteenth pastor of St. Mary's Church. Of these three titles (Christian, priest, and pastor), the most important by far for my salvation is the first: I am a disciple of Jesus Christ. . . .*

*My friends, we are here today because the Son of Mary is the Son of God: the Alpha and the Omega, the First and the Last, the Beginning and the End. He it is through whom, by whom, and for whom all things were made. Jesus Christ is the answer to which every human life is the question, and only by knowing, loving, and serving Jesus Christ can we fulfill the deepest desires of our hearts.*

*. . . I have not always been a Christian. To the horror of my Protestant family, I became an atheist at the age of thirteen, and until I was nineteen I remained sincerely convinced that there is no God, that the cosmos could be explained without a creator. In October of 1981, however, during my sophomore year at Princeton, I discovered my error. The Lord Jesus Christ laid hold of my life on the evening of October 15, and here I am today to bear witness to the power of his love. Since that moment, the gospel of Christ has been my consuming passion, and I want it to be yours as well. . . .*

*If Jesus Christ is Lord, then he is Lord of everything—of all that we are and all that we have. In the coming years of my service here, we will explore together the inexhaustible riches of the Incarnate Word who calls us by our baptism to follow him unreservedly. . . .*

*During all the years of my formation, I struggled to understand how and why God had called me; at length, though, the time of testing and trial came to an end, and on July 10th, 1993, I was ordained to the Priesthood of Jesus Christ for the Diocese of Charleston. Since then I have been a college chaplain, a parish priest, and most recently a seminary professor, and despite the wide variety of work in those jobs, in each of my posts my fundamental duties have been the same: to teach, to sanctify, and to govern. These three duties remain with a priest no matter what work he may be engaged in because they flow not from what he does, but from what he is. Presbyteral ordination configures the man ordained to the Person of Christ the Head and Bridegroom of the Church in such a way that he is able to stand in the Person of Christ and act in his name for the welfare of the whole Church . . .*

*. . . [Our] first church was dedicated in 1876 in the month of October; you may recall that my conversion to Christ also occurred in October, 105 years later. [The diocesan] archives revealed to me something more: both events took place on the same day, the 15th of October. My friends, I believe that everything in my life to date has been in some way a preparation for*

> *the work I am now beginning here, and words cannot convey the joy I feel to be your pastor. Twenty years ago, the Blessed Virgin Mary, Christ's first and greatest disciple, led me to embrace with faith and love the Sacred Heart of her divine Son, and now she has guided me here to lead a congregation dedicated in her honor on the day of my conversion to the Sacred Heart of her divine Son. There are no mere coincidences in God, and so I am certain that my service here is meant to be a privileged moment of grace in my life. I pray most fervently that it may be the same for you. . . .*
>
> *I pledge to you today my solemn commitment to love you as a shepherd, to teach you as a father, and to walk with you as a brother in the daily struggle to answer the call of Christ: "Follow me."*

At which point, we may safely conclude, the people of St. Mary's Parish in Greenville, South Carolina, knew that it wasn't going to be business-as-usual with Father Jay Scott Newman.

---

On June 22, 2003, Corpus Christi Sunday, the parishioners of St. Mary's, Greenville, packed the church for a Solemn Mass. In a little less than two years, the church and its campus had been transformed. The brick had been repointed and the pews refinished; the stained glass had been cleaned, the interior of the church had been completely repainted, and a glorious new golden tabernacle had been installed. A large carved oaken ambo had been built to complement the restored oaken reredos and provide a fitting place for the proclamation of Scripture and preaching. The baptismal font had been moved to the front door, so that those entering the Church could remind themselves, every week or indeed every day, of who they were and why they were there. The entire parish campus had been relandscaped. Amid an economic down tick, the people of St. Mary's had cheerfully given $2 million to have all this done, and more.

But if you'd been there that day, what would have struck you most powerfully would have been how the congregation itself had been transformed. More than six hundred people lustily sang three classic hymns: "At the Lamb's High Feast We Sing," "Alleluia! Sing to Jesus," and the Latin motet *Adoro Te Devote*; the choir sang Cesar Franck's *Panis Angelicus* and William Byrd's *Ave Verum Corpus*; both congregation and choir were accompanied by organ, trumpet, tympani, violin, and viola. The congregation had learned to chant its proper parts of the Mass—the Kyrie, the Gloria, the Sanctus, the Memorial Acclamation after the consecration, the Lord's Prayer, and the Agnus Dei. Everyone sang the antiphon to the psalm response between the first and second readings, and the priest-celebrant's exchanges with the congregation ("The Lord be with you," etc.) were also sung. Laymen read the Old and New Testament Scriptures clearly and reverently, and processed the gifts of bread and wine to the altar. Everyone's attention was riveted as Father Newman sang most of the Eucharistic Prayer in a simple chant that underscored the solemnity of this central action of the Mass.

What with a chanted Sequence (a long poem that sets the stage for the proclamation of the Gospel on special feast days and is usually omitted in most parishes), plus an appeal from a visiting missionary, plus the blessing of a seminarian leaving for Rome, the Mass lasted an hour and forty-five minutes. When it was over, everyone present was disappointed that they'd finished so soon.

Why? Because in his first months as pastor of St. Mary's, Father Newman had restored to his people their baptismal dignity as Christians. Liturgy at many Catholic parishes (as I expect you know) is often a quickie, forty-five minute affair—"Suburban Lite," as some clerical wags describe it. That's not what happens in Greenville, and there are no complaints. I don't think the reason why can be reduced to the splendid music and the exemplary preaching. Rather, the people of St. Mary's, who are quite ordinary people (as the world judges these things), have come to understand themselves differently. They now know that they are men and women empowered by Christ in baptism to offer true worship to the Father.

In 1963 the bishops of the Second Vatican Council taught that the liturgy we celebrate here and now is a participation in "the heavenly liturgy which is celebrated in the Holy City of Jerusalem toward which we journey as pilgrims, where Christ is sitting at the right hand of God, minister of the holies and of the true tabernacle." The people of St. Mary's, Greenville, might not be able to tell you exactly what that high theological language means. But in a sense they don't have to; they *know* what it means, in their hearts and minds and souls, from their experience. They know that they don't leave church on Sunday morning to return to the "real world." They know that, at Mass on Sunday, they're *in* the real world—the really real world of communion with God.

They understand intuitively and experientially what Angelo Scola, the patriarch of Venice and a fine theologian, meant when he said a few years ago that the sacraments, and preeminently the Eucharist, are where we encounter Christ "as his contemporary."

You know, as every Catholic knows, that the liturgy has been a battleground in the Church since Vatican II. A lot of arguments about the way Catholics worship and pray have to do with tastes and aesthetics. But the deeper arguments have to do with different ideas of what worship is. And that's serious.

As the Catholic Church understands it, the liturgy is God's work, not our work. It's our participation, here and now, in what is already and always happening around the Throne of Grace, where angels and saints sing the praises of God forever. To say that the liturgy isn't "our work" doesn't mean that priests and people don't have a lot to do with what goes on at Mass; they obviously do, and some, like the people of St. Mary's, Greenville, and their pastor, do their parts with great care, reverence, and good taste. The liturgy at Greenville, however, is a powerful experience because everyone involved knows that God is the real author of our worship. In the liturgy restored and renewed as Vatican II intended, the people of Greenville have come to understand that it is God who invites us to worship and empowers us to worship.

Lots of young Catholics complain that they're bored at Mass. I don't blame them. When priests and people forget what's really going on here—when the Mass is another form of entertainment, or therapy, or even therapeutic entertainment—the Mass is not what it's meant to be—and we're not what we were meant to be, in our baptism. So here's the basic point, which is a countercultural point: *We don't worship God because it makes us feel good, or relieved, or entertained. We worship God because God is to be worshiped—and in giving God the worship that is his due, we satisfy one of the deepest longings of the human spirit.*

Which means that to participate in the Mass here and now is not a matter of looking down or looking around, but of looking up—it's a taste of what awaits us, through the grace and mercy of God, for all eternity. True worship, like true love, doesn't mean looking into each other's eyes; it means looking together, in love, at the One who is Love all the way through.

---

Why is the way we worship—and what we understand our worship to mean—so important? Another Greenville story: In his first few months in St. Mary's Parish, Father Newman went to a coffee in the home of parishioners every Monday night. There he explained why, as he put it, "I don't believe in living room liturgy." This wasn't a matter of taste or a question of power. It was a matter of the right way to worship God—the right way to live the noble calling that is every Christian's by baptism.

The people of St. Mary's Greenville have learned experientially an ancient theological maxim that you should know: *lex orandi lex credendi*—what we pray is what we believe. Sloppy worship leads inevitably to sloppy theology. Worship-as-entertainment dumbs down the truths that true worship celebrates. In the past thirty-five years, according to some serious survey research, more than a few Catholics have begun to lose their grip on the truth that what we receive in the Eucharist is the body and blood of Christ. Can anyone seriously argue that that erosion of belief doesn't have something to do with sloppy liturgy, in which the focal point of worship too often becomes the congregation itself or the Phil Donahue–style priest-"presider" (to use the most hideous trope in contemporary liturgical jargon)?

My friend Robert Louis Wilken, a distinguished scholar of the early Church, once told a reporter why he had entered into full communion with the Catholic Church in his sixties, after a lifetime as a serious Lutheran and decades as a Lutheran pastor. For Wilken, a historian and theologian, it finally came down to a question of what preserved the faith over time. What keeps us in touch, in communion, with the Church's apostolic roots, which we explored in the *scavi* of St. Peter's in Rome? The Reformation tradition in which Wilken grew up believed that it could preserve the apostolic faith through a firm adherence to doctrine. The Catholic counterview, which Wilken finally found irrefutable, was that the community of the Church—the community in which doctrine comes to be understood as doctrine—preserves the faith. One powerful example of that touched this maxim, *lex orandi lex credendi.*

During the controversies of the Reformation and Counter-Reformation, there was a famous debate between a Lutheran theologian and St. Robert Bellarmine. As Wilken remembered the story, the Lutheran argued against the Catholic practice of Eucharistic reservation and adoration—preserving elements of the Eucharist in a tabernacle before which the faithful would pray—on the grounds that Christ intended the Eucharist to be used, not reserved: "take and eat," not "take and reserve," so to speak. Bellermine's counter was that the Church had been reserving the sacrament for a long time and there wasn't any serious reason to stop the practice. Over time, Wilken admitted, jettisoning the tabernacle and the reserved sacrament had led many Lutherans to a different and diminished Eucharistic theology, uncertain about Christ's real presence in the bread and wine. Catholics kept their tabernacles and sustained the practice of Eucharistic reservation and adoration. Traditional practice—the Catholic community and the way it worshiped—had preserved a key truth of Catholic faith.

Which gives you some sense, not only of what *lex orandi lex credendi* means, but of why Father Newman moved the tabernacle back to the center of the sanctuary of St. Mary's, Greenville, fifteen minutes after arriving in the parish.

The Catholic Church has failed its Lord times beyond numbering. "Do this in memory of me" is the commandment of Christ to which the Church has been most faithful. The Eucharist, celebrated at Mass and reserved in order to extend the fruits of the Mass through time, keeps the Church faithful. That's why *lex orandi lex credendi* is so important. And that's why today's liturgical tong wars in the Catholic Church are worth fighting. A lot more is at stake here than questions of taste.

---

While we're on the subject of worship and liturgy, let's think for a minute about what a Catholic priest is. There's more than a little confusion on the subject. Centuries of legalization in the Church, compounded by the bureaucratization that affects just about every aspect of modern life, has led a lot of Catholics, clerical and lay, to think of the priest as a kind of ecclesiastical functionary—a man licensed by the hierarchy to do certain kinds of church business. The Second Vatican Council tried to remedy this by reminding Catholics that there is only one High Priest, Jesus Christ, in whose unique exercise of the priesthood every Christian shares by baptism—precisely the truth about themselves that the people of St. Mary's, Greenville, have rediscovered through Father Newman. At the same time, the council taught that the ordained priesthood is not just a set of functions or tasks within what theologians call the "common priesthood" of all the baptized. Nor does the ordained priest "represent" this common priesthood in the way, for example, a congressman represents his district—the ordained priest isn't a stand-in for the priestly community that is the whole Church.

Rather, the Catholic Church teaches that *the ordained priest is an icon of the eternal priesthood of Jesus Christ*—someone who by the grace of his ordination, not by his own merits, *makes Christ present* in his person. That's why an older generation of Catholics were taught that a priest is an *alter Christus*, "another Christ," and that a priest acts *in persona Christi*, "in the person of Christ." Remember our earlier discussion about the difference between a "symbol" and a "sign"? That distinction applies here. The ordained priest is an ordinary man who has been made, by the power of God, into an extraordinary symbol—a re-presentation—of Christ the High Priest of his people.

And that brings us to clericalism. Priestly fraternity and fellowship is one of the great goods of Catholic life. Yet when fellowship and fraternity decay into clericalism and the Church gets divided into castes, something has gone wrong. The Catholic priesthood doesn't exist as a kind of clerical caste for its own sake. In the Catholic Church, the ordained priesthood lifts up and ennobles the "common priesthood" of all the people of the Church. That is what the priest does, as Father Newman put it in his inaugural sermon, by teaching, sanctifying, and governing his people. That governance is a matter of service, not power, because a man is ordained as a servant, not as a petty parochial dictator. At the same time, and by the same token, one service the priest does his people is to exercise pastoral authority—not, again, for its own sake, but to empower the people given into his care. Empower them to do what? To realize in their prayer and worship and daily life the truth about themselves as men and women who have been touched with the fire of the Holy Spirit in baptism and confirmation; men and women who can worship God and receive the body and blood of the Son of God in holy communion; men and women called and sent into the world as witnesses and servants.

This "iconography" of the priesthood has a body language built into it—which brings us to another thorny issue: who can be ordained? But perhaps now you can begin to see how this issue, so often positioned as a question of power, is in fact a question that engages some very deep truths about the ordinary and the extraordinary, the visible and the invisible, the mundane and the transcendent.

As we've discussed before, maleness and femaleness are not accidents of evolutionary biology in the Catholic sacramental imagination. Rather, our maleness and femaleness are iconographic—visible, earthy realities through which we learn some important truths about our humanity and about God (just as we saw in the Sistine Chapel). Men and women are radically equal in being images of God. But men and women are not interchangeable icons of God's presence in his creation. The Catholic Church takes our sexual embodiedness as male and female very seriously—far more seriously than the modern gnostics who reduce "male" and "female" to constructs of culture.

In the first and second generations of the Church, Christians came to understand something very important: *Christ's relationship to the Church is spousal, or nuptial.* As Ephesians 5:25 puts it, Christ loves the Church as a husband loves a wife. That complete giving of self is most powerfully evident at Mass, when the priest, acting in the person of Christ, makes the Lord's gift of himself present in a way that we can see and touch and taste by consecrating the bread and wine that become Christ's body and blood.

In a Christian community in which the Lord's Supper is a memorial meal, it makes no difference whether the one who presides at this exercise in table fellowship is a man or a woman; it's simply a question of custom, because here the "ministry" is functional, not sacramental. But that's not what Catholics understand by the Lord's Supper—the Eucharist—or by the priesthood. In the Catholic sacramental imagination, remember, *stuff counts*—including the stuff of being male or female. If the Eucharist is the most intense "making present" of Christ's spousal gift of himself to his bride, the Church, then a priest who can make Christ present precisely in this male donation of self to spouse is required.

Tough stuff in our unisex culture, I know. But consider the possibility that this way of thinking about things takes femaleness and maleness far more seriously than the postmodern academic crazies who reduce our embodiedness to a question of plumbing. When the Catholic Church ordains men to the priesthood, it isn't engaging in misogyny and it isn't violating anyone's "rights"—no one, from the pope to the humblest parish priest, ever had a "right" to be ordained a priest. Rather, the Church is being serious about embodiedness and what that means. It's living its commitment to the sacramentality of the world.

---

Thinking about liturgy—the public worship of the Church—leads naturally enough to thinking about prayer. As I've said to you before, Christianity isn't "spirituality" of the sort that you find stocked under that rubric in your local Barnes & Noble. Christianity isn't about our search for God; Christianity is about God's search for us in history, and our taking the path God has taken. If that's what Christianity *is*, then Christian prayer must have something to do with that.

Do you remember the story of Jesus and the Samaritan woman he meets at a well? It's in the fourth chapter St. John's Gospel, and it's interesting that the *Catechism of the Catholic Church* uses this episode to begin its teaching about prayer. The Samaritan woman comes to Jacob's well to draw water and finds Jesus, a Jew, sitting there. She doesn't expect anything in the way of greeting or courtesy; Jews don't talk to Samaritans. But this Jew does. "Give me a drink," Jesus asks her. Then they begin to talk and, as the old spiritual has it, "he told her everything she'd ever done." The point isn't Jesus' insight into the Samaritan woman's tangled personal affairs and spiritual life, however. It's the way the story is set up.

Jesus' request for a drink and the woman's final response at the end of the tale—"Come, see a man who told me all I ever did. Can this be the Christ?"—teaches us something important about the surprising nature of prayer: *Prayer begins with God's thirst for us*. "Give me a drink." Prayer is the meeting place between God's thirst, God's desire, for us and our heart's yearning for God. As the *Catechism* puts it, "God thirsts that we may thirst for him." We can pray because the Spirit is in us, causing us to thirst for God; and the Holy Spirit has been given to us because of God's thirst for us. *Prayer isn't something we initiate*. Prayer is a meeting with the Christ who always takes the initiative, as he did at Jacob's well with the Samaritan woman. For she is all of us: "The wonder of prayer is revealed beside the well where we come seeking water; there, Christ comes to meet every human being. It is he who first seeks us and asks us for a drink. Jesus thirsts; his asking arises from the depths of God's desire for us."

There's a virtual infinity of ways to pray as a Catholic. I've talked at length here about the Mass, and why a place like St. Mary's, Greenville, answers that perennial question, Why should I go to church? To which the answer is, Go to a place like St. Mary's, Greenville, and the question will answer itself. I've talked a bit about the rosary as a way of prayer that embodies Mary's unique role in salvation history as the first disciple who always points beyond herself to her son—"Do whatever he tells you." There are many, many forms of Catholic devotion, but there's one other major form of Catholic prayer I haven't mentioned—the Liturgy of the Hours, also known as the Divine Office.

Catholicism is about time as well as space, history as well as stuff. Time counts, just as stuff counts, in the sacramental imagination. That's why the Church has a liturgy of the *hours*, a daily routine of prescribed prayer—to sanctify time, to take time seriously. The Liturgy of the Hours pivots around Lauds, or "Morning Prayer," and Vespers, or "Evening Prayer." Both Lauds and Vespers are composed of a hymn, psalms and Old Testament canticles, a Bible reading, a Gospel canticle, intercessory prayers, the Lord's Prayer, and a concluding prayer or collect. In the reformed Liturgy of the Hours, the old office of "Matins" or "Vigils," which can be said at any time of the day, has become the "Office of Readings," where lengthier Scripture readings and readings from great theologians and spiritual masters are on tap. There are shorter "hours" at three times during the day, and the whole business concludes with Compline or "Night Prayer." After a psalm or two and a very brief reading, the Church's daily prayer ends with the *nunc dimittis* of aged Simeon in the New Testament ("Now, Lord, you may dismiss your servant in peace, according to your word" [Luke 2:29–32]) and a hymn to the Virgin Mary.

All men in holy orders are obliged to pray the Liturgy of the Hours every day. Cloistered religious women and men make "the office" the structure of their day, and many active religious communities (teachers, health care workers, etc.) bind themselves to the Liturgy of the Hours, too—as do a surprising number of laypeople, including younger people. I've made "the office" the basic structure of my daily prayer for almost twenty years, saying Lauds every morning and Vespers and Compline every evening. When I'm living in a religious house (as when I lived at the North American College in Rome while researching *Witness to Hope*), it's a great pleasure to pray the office in community; but it's also entirely possible to pray it alone, which is what I do most of the time. And while there are certainly dry spells from time to time, I really wouldn't know how to live without that daily routine.

There's a good way to ease yourself into a daily routine of prayer, however, and that's to get a subscription to *Magnificat*, a monthly prayer book that has been one of the astonishing successes in the Catholic Church in recent years. *Magnificat*, which is beautiful as well as handy, is both a missal with all the Mass texts for the month (so that you can join in the Church's reflection at Mass each day even if you can't attend) as well as a shortened form of "the office"—modified morning, evening, and night prayer. Each monthly issue also includes wonderfully interesting lives of the saints (from a seemingly bottomless treasure trove of Catholic historical trivia) and brief spiritual readings, some by contemporary authors and others from the Catholic classics. You can fit it into a suit jacket pocket or a purse. It's simply the best way I know to get some structure into your daily prayer. A lot of people seem to find it helpful—from a standing start, *Magnificat* has attracted more than 150,000 subscribers in the United States alone in four years. You can check it out at www.magnificat.net. It's worth a look, as a reminder that beauty and regularity are important elements of worship.

Which reminds us, again, the worship isn't something we make up. To which the only appropriate response is—thank God.

# 10

## St. Stanisław Kostka Churchyard, Warsaw/The Metropolitan Curia, Kraków—How Vocations Change History

There are some important things to learn about what it means to be Catholic—and what being Catholic means to history—in what's arguably the most intensely Catholic country in the world: Poland.

Poland is a land of shrines and pilgrimage. The vast outdoor Holy Land shrine southwest of Kraków, Kalwaria Zebrzydowska, covers hundreds of acres of Galician woodland and draws tens of thousands of pilgrims every year, just as it has for centuries. Down in the Tatras, in Zakopane, you can visit one of the newest Polish shrines, an A-frame basilica built in Polish mountaineer style and dedicated to Our Lady of Fatima, in thanksgiving for her having spared the life of Pope John Paul II when he was shot in 1981—a Marian intervention that the *gorale*, the Polish highlanders, believe is as obvious a fact of history as King Jan Sobieski's beating the Turks at Vienna in 1683. Then there's Wawel Cathedral in Kraków, magnetic pole of the country's emotional life, where many of Poland's heroes (including Sobieski) are buried. The greatest of Polish shrines is the Jasna Góra monastery in Częstochowa, home of a famous icon, the Black Madonna. On this Polish part of our tour, I hope you'll come to love her as I do. But let's not start, or even end up, at Jasna Góra or any of the other, more obvious places. Rather, let's go to sites that aren't shrines in any formal sense—a parish churchyard in Warsaw; a house and an apartment building and the bishop's residence in Kraków. In each of these places, young Catholics, not unlike you, made decisions about their vocations.

Those decisions helped change the course of modern history.

---

Warsaw isn't a very lovely or lovable city. If you saw the recent movie about the Warsaw Ghetto, *The Pianist*, you know that Hitler ordered the city flattened, building by building and block by block, in retaliation for the 1944 Warsaw Uprising. Having your capital city completely leveled is bad enough; having it rebuilt by communists is another form of insult. When I first went there in 1991, Warsaw was a gray, dull place. Unimaginative architecture, shoddy construction, and forty-five years of deferred maintenance made for almost unrelieved dreariness. Things have changed over the past decade and downtown Warsaw is lively, even if its new buildings make you think of Dallas or Houston.

I've been to Poland dozens of times, but that first visit, in 1991, was something of a pilgrimage, at least as I think back on it. On a flight back from Moscow in October 1990, I had gotten the idea into my head that the Catholic Church had had something to do with the collapse of European communism—and I came to Poland eight months later to test that intuition by talking with the people who had made the Revolution of 1989. Shortly after I arrived in Warsaw, I felt an irresistible tug drawing me to the churchyard of St. Stanisław Kostka, in the Żoliborz district.

Żoliborz is a fifteen- or twenty-minute tram ride from downtown. Today, as for decades, it's a traditionally bohemian area, leaning to the port side in its politics; in the 1960s and 1970s, I'm told, Żoliborz was one of the few places in Poland where you could find an intellectually respectable Marxist to argue with. The tram lets you off at a roundabout that was known, between 1946 and 1991, by an ungainly communist moniker—Square of the Defense of the Paris Commune. By 1991, and thanks to what happened in 1989, it had reverted to the name it bore in the 1920s and 1930s: Woodrow Wilson Square. As you walk through the square you can see, off to the left, a steeple. Head in that direction and you'll find yourself, in a couple of blocks, at the Church of St. Stanisław Kostka.

In the churchyard, you'll see a tremendous granite cross, perhaps ten feet long, lying on the ground, its polished surface reflecting the clouds and trees above. The churchyard is rimmed by large, unpolished stones, each joined to its neighbor by iron links. Then you notice that the linked stones are joined to the top of the great granite cross. And suddenly it becomes clear—this is a rosary.

Buried underneath the granite cross is Father Jerzy Popiełuszko. Many, myself included, consider him a contemporary martyr.

Father Jerzy, which is "George" *po Polsku*, was thirty-four years old when Poland's communist government declared martial law in December 1981, in an attempt to crush the Solidarity trade union—which was, as everyone understood and nobody could admit, a political opposition as well as a workers movement. Popiełuszko (pronounced pop-ee-WHOOSH-koe) hadn't had a very distinguished ecclesiastical career up to that point. He hadn't been a prodigy in the seminary. His health was chronically poor, he was thin as a rail, and he had a weak pulpit voice.

In August 1980, the month that Solidarity exploded into life in the deliciously named "Lenin" shipyards at Gdańsk on Poland's Baltic coast, Cardinal Stefan Wyszyński, the primate of Poland and Father Jerzy's superior, named the young priest a chaplain to workers at a Warsaw steel mill; the workers were striking in support of what was happening in Gdańsk. Week after week, as the drama of Solidarity played itself out in 1980 and 1981, Father Jerzy celebrated Mass, heard confessions, and counseled with the steelworkers. Then martial law struck on the night of December 12–13, 1981. The Polish state invaded the Polish nation, using the Polish army as its weapon.

A month later, Father Jerzy Popiełuszko began a monthly "Mass for the Fatherland" at St. Stanisław Kostka, the Żoliborz church where he was assigned as a very junior curate. At those Masses, this quiet, previously unassuming priest found a voice—and perhaps new meaning in his priestly vocation. There was no rabble-rousing. But Father Jerzy's quiet eloquence soon had hundreds, then thousands, and finally tens of thousands packing into and around St. Stanisław Kostka for the monthly "Mass for the Fatherland." It made no difference whether it was hot or cold, dry or wet, or whether snow blanketed the ground. People came. And Father Jerzy challenged them.

He took his theme, relentlessly repeated, from Pope John Paul II: "vanquish evil with good." He preached nonviolence. But he also preached the moral duty of resistance. In his quiet, urgent way, Father Jerzy was asking his people, "Whose side will you take? The side of good, or the side of evil? Truth or falsehood? Love or hatred?" Father Jerzy wasn't a theological sophisticate, and he wasn't a political theorist. He was something more—a man who could inspire others to the moral heroism he displayed himself. Michael Kaufman, then Warsaw bureau chief for the *New York Times*, quickly grasped how dramatic, defiant, and unique all of this was: "Nowhere else from East Berlin to Vladivostok could anyone stand before ten or fifteen thousand people and use a microphone to condemn the errors of state and party. Nowhere, in that vast stretch encompassing some four hundred million people was anyone else telling a crowd that defiance of authority was an obligation of the heart, of religion, of manhood, and of nationhood."

The *Times* chief in Poland wasn't the only one who understood, though. So did the SB, the Polish secret police. That's why they decided to kill Father Jerzy Popiełuszko.

Driving back to Warsaw from a pastoral assignment in Bydgoszcz on October 19, 1984, Father Jerzy was pulled over by three SB officers. They trussed him up, beat him to death with their fists, their feet, and their bludgeons, and then threw his battered corpse into the Vistula River near Włocławek. The next day, the state radio announced that Father Jerzy Popiełuszko had disappeared and was presumed kidnapped by "unknown parties." People began flocking to the Żoliborz churchyard by the tens of thousands, from all over the country. Masses were offered every hour, around the clock. This went on for ten days. Then, on October 30, came the news that everyone simultaneously feared and expected—the body of Father Jerzy Popiełuszko had been dredged out of the Vistula.

The announcement was made in the midst of a Mass at St. Stanisław Kostka. Another of the Żoliborz priests, Father Antonin Lewek, a friend of Father Jerzy, urged the vast congregation to remember Jesus at the death of Lazarus—to cry but not to strike out in violent anger. Then, Father Lewek remembered, something extraordinary happened: three times the crowd, in tears, repeated after the priests concelebrating the Mass, "And forgive us our trespasses as we forgive those who trespass against us. And forgive us our trespasses as we forgive . . . "

Normal practice would have called for Popiełuszko to be buried in Warsaw's Powazki cemetery, but ten thousand of Father Jerzy's steelworkers signed a petition to the new primate, Cardinal Józef Glemp, asking that he allow Father Jerzy to be buried in the churchyard at St. Stanisław Kostka, a few yards from where he had celebrated the Masses for the Fatherland and called his people to live in the truth. After the slain priest's mother intervened, the cardinal agreed. With several hundred thousand Warsawians in the streets that day, Father Jerzy was laid to rest in his churchyard on November 3, 1984.

The churchyard instantly became a shrine, "a little piece of free Poland," as one Solidarity activist put it to me in 1991. This was "Solidarity's sanctuary," a place of prayer and reflection that carried on the work Father Jerzy had begun from the pulpit inside the church. In his sermons, he had told his people that "one cannot murder hopes." Five years after his death, his hopes, and those of millions of other Poles, were vindicated in the Revolution of 1989. No one who ever visited the churchyard in Żoliborz could doubt that Father Jerzy was watching those epic events, if from a different vantage point.

---

The cause for the beatification of Father Jerzy Popiełuszko is under way. If that process comes to fruition, it will confirm what many people who knew him, and many more who didn't, already believe—this was a saintly man. There are many different kinds of sanctity in the Church. Hans Urs von Balthasar once wrote that some saints are "God's prime numbers," men and women who blaze new trails in holiness or have unique Christian personalities: Francis of Assisi, for example. Other saints lead exemplary lives that run along more conventional spiritual tracks. In either case, the "prime numbers" or the exemplars, it's important to understand that the Church doesn't make saints; God makes saints. The Church recognizes publicly the saints that God has made.

Father Jerzy Popiełuszko's sanctity unfolded in very distinctive circumstances. In the ninth decade of a century of lethal lies, he embodied the sanctity of integrity. Father Jerzy was in no sense a born revolutionary. But when the moment came, he knew how to speak truth to power, and he knew how to do it in ways that summoned others to a similar truth-telling—without violence but without compromise, either.

Things were very, very dicey in Poland in the early 1980s. The situation could easily have gotten out of hand; if it had, the Soviet Union might have invaded, with untold consequences in Europe and around the world. But events didn't spiral out of control. Solidarity changed Poland (indeed, Solidarity helped change all of central and eastern Europe) through means other than the usual twentieth-century method of large-scale social change—mass slaughter. That was due in no small part to the courage and the conviction of people like Father Jerzy Popiełuszko. Without him, and others like him, things could have been very different indeed, for all of us.

So we come here to honor a man of courage. But we also come here because Father Jerzy's story teaches us several other important things about Catholic faith and its practice. *Faith has consequences*. At the personal level, those consequences are vocational—What is it that I am called to do? How do I live the truth of who I am? When he entered the seminary, young Jerzy Popiełuszko hadn't the slightest idea of becoming a world figure, much less a martyr. He was a quiet, retiring, pious lad who may have seen the priesthood as a place to be, well, quiet and retiring and pious. Yet he lived out, to the very end, the truth of what he had been ordained to be. And that had consequences, not only for him personally but for the people whose lives he touched—people through whom he helped change history. Faith has consequences for history, too.

That's an old Catholic idea, nowhere more clearly expressed than by the great English historian Christopher Dawson, reflecting on the fact that one of the most decisive moments in European history was completely ignored by the historians of the time:

> *When St. Paul, in obedience to the warning of a dream, set sail from Troy in* A.D. *49 and came to Philippi in Macedonia he did more to change the course of history than the great battle that had decided the fate of the Roman Empire on the same spot a century earlier, for he brought to Europe the seed of a new life which was ultimately destined to create a new world. All this took place underneath the surface of history, so that it was unrecognized by the leaders of contemporary culture . . . who actually saw it taking place beneath their eyes.*

"Underneath the surface of history"—that's where Catholic faith has its deepest consequences. Yes, the Catholic Church appears time and again on the "surface" of history. But what's often of more enduring consequence is taking place below-the-radar-screen, as it were. It's happening in minds and hearts and souls, in vocational choices and decisions.

And that brings us south, to a much lovelier and more lovable city, Kraków, ancient capital of royal Poland and the center of the country's cultural life for hundreds of years. Here, from 1939 through 1946, things were happening "underneath the surface of history"—things that eventually changed the story line of the late twentieth century.

Pope John Paul II is the first pope in a long time to tell us that he had a hard time making a vocational decision for the priesthood. Yet he did. When Karol Wojtyła moved to Kraków with his pensioner father in 1938 to begin his studies in Polish philology at the Jagiellonian University, he didn't think he was going to be a priest; he thought he was going to be an actor, a man of the theater, with perhaps a parallel career in academic life. As he put it in a memoir published in 1996, he was "completely absorbed by a passion for literature, especially dramatic literature, and for the theater." It wasn't simply a question of that passion leaving little or no room for a priestly vocation; young Karol Wojtyła's passion for literature and the theater seemed to him to be his vocation.

Then things changed. And so did Karol Wojtyła.

The brutal German occupation of Poland, from September 1939 through January 1945, was the biblical fiery furnace in which Karol Wojtyła's vocation was clarified and purified. The long-term German strategy for Poland was simple: the Poles were to be erased as a race of subhumans. In the interim, they were to work for the greater glory of the Third Reich, subsisting on a minimal diet. Hitler knew that the Poles wouldn't truckle quietly; alone, after all, the Poles in 1939 had held out against the Wehrmacht for three weeks longer than the French managed to do, with British air and ground support, in 1940. So Poland was divided. Its eastern borderlands were handed over to Stalin (his reward for the cynical Molotov-Ribbentrop Pact of August 1939); western Polish areas were annexed to the German Reich (thus the Polish town of Oświęcim was renamed "Auschwitz"); and the great center of the country became what historian Norman Davies calls "Gestapoland." Styled the "General Gouvernement" and run from Krakow's Wawel Castle by a political gangster named Hans Frank, it was an area in which the rule of law ceased to exist and a reign of terror ensued. This was where Karol Wojtyła lived from age nineteen through age twenty-four.

In Hans Frank's Gestapoland, the initial occupation strategy was to decapitate any possible Polish resistance by decapitating Polish culture. The Nazis shut down the Jagiellonian University and shipped many of its most distinguished professors off to the Sachsenhausen concentration camp. Polish cultural life went underground; it was a capital crime to be caught playing Chopin, and Poles of courage and conviction defied the German effort to destroy their cultural memory at the daily risk of their lives. Young Wojtyła was one of them. He took clandestine courses as the Jagiellonian reorganized itself as an underground school. He helped found a theatrical group that believed in resistance-through-drama: the Rhapsodic Theater, which worked to keep Poland's memory alive by performing the classics of the Polish stage and Polish poetry. At the same time, young Karol worked as a manual laborer, first in a stone quarry, later in a chemical factory, walking to work in freezing winter weather in denims and clogs, trying to scrounge something to eat for his father and himself on his way home in the evening.

If you walk through Kraków's Old Town toward Wawel Castle and cathedral and then turn right, you'll find yourself walking, as Karol Wojtyła did, along the embankment of the Vistula River. Cross the first bridge you come to and you'll be in the working-class neighborhood, Dębniki, where young Karol Wojtyła wrestled with the question of what he was supposed to do with his life. Tyniecka Street borders the embankment on the Dębniki side of the Vistula; if you walk a few hundred yards down the street, you'll come to Tyniecka 10, a three-story house where Karol lived from 1938 to 1944. Here in the dark, damp basement apartment his friends called "The Catacomb" the Rhapsodic Theater was launched and held rehearsals. Here Karol's father died on February 18, 1941; here young Karol spent a night in prayer beside his father's body, remembering later that "I never felt so alone." Here he asked himself a question he remembered a half century later: "So many people of my own age are losing their lives, *why not me*?"

And here he read the works of the great Carmelite mystics, St. John of the Cross and St. Teresa of Avila. They had been lent to him by a surprising character, a man he came to call the "unexpected apostle"—Jan Tyranowski. He was a forty-something bachelor, a tailor by training, who lived in another part of Dębniki at 11 Różana Street. He spent the early hours of each day at his trade, and the rest of the day in a life of meditation and prayer more rigorous than that led by many monks or nuns. When the Gestapo arrested most of the Salesian fathers at the Dębniki parish, the remaining priest asked Tyranowski to take over what we would now call the parish "youth ministry" to young men. Tyranowski began forming the young men of Dębniki into what he called "Living Rosary" groups, fifteen to a group, with a more mature youngster as the group leader or "animator." Karol Wojtyła was one of the first "animators" of the Living Rosary. Tyranowski must have sensed that this literary young man would be attracted to the poetry of John of the Cross and the drama of Teresa of Avila's rambunctious life, and he introduced Karol Wojtyła to these sixteenth-century Spanish mystics: St. Teresa's *Autobiography*; St. John's *Dark Night of the Soul*, *Spiritual Canticle*, *Ascent of Mt. Carmel*, and *Living Flame of Love*. Carmelite mysticism is a spirituality of abandonment, focused on the crucified Christ, dying in complete self-abnegation and abandonment to the will of his Father. Reading St. John and St. Teresa under the tutelage of Jan Tyranowski, it's not hard to imagine Karol Wojtyła saying, as Edith Stein had in the 1920s when reading Teresa's autobiography, "This is the truth."

Back in "The Catacomb" and while lugging buckets of lime during the night shift at the Solway chemical plant in Borek Fałęcki, Karol wrestled with that truth, with himself, and with God for several months after his father's death. According to the Carmelite mystics, we can only know God in himself when we give up all our human attempts to "reach" God by our own striving—when we, like Jesus, abandon ourselves in an act of complete self-surrender, which is a radical act of love. It would be hard to imagine a way of thinking more different from the Nazi exaltation of the "triumph of the will," which was then killing Karol's friends and colleagues day by day on the streets of Kraków.

As 1941 gave way to 1942, something was happening in the soul of Karol Wojtyła. Abandoning himself to the will of God was slowly becoming the defining characteristic of his discipleship. Like carbon deposits deep beneath the earth, he was being hard pressed by turbulent forces. And, as sometimes happens with carbon, those powerful forces were forming him into a diamond, something brilliant and hard, able to cut through the seemingly impenetrable.

He made his decision in the fall of 1942. It wasn't a matter of choosing the priesthood, as he would have chosen the theater or the academic life. It was a question of coming to recognize that he had been chosen—and to that choosing there could only be one answer. Karol's decision led him to the great house and diocesan office complex at Franciszkańska 3 on the border of Krakow's Old Town. This was the residence of the archbishops of the city, known to one and all as the "Metropolitan Curia." The Nazis shut down the seminary shortly after seizing power, but the courageous archbishop, Adam Stefan Sapieha, reconstituted the seminary underground. Karol Wojtyła now became a clandestine seminarian, working at the Solway plant, studying on the side, quietly slipping in and out of Franciszkańska 3 for exams, further reading assignments, and counsel. (Looking across Franciszkańska Street from the Metropolitan Curia today, you can see a statue of Cardinal Sapieha that Karol Wojtyła, then archbishop himself, commissioned in the 1970s. The cardinal seems to be looking down into hell, and the inscription on the stone base of the bronze statue describes him as "the archbishop of the long, dark night of Occupation." The Carmelite allusion isn't accidental.) Karol would also come to Franciszkańska 3 to serve the archbishop's early morning Mass, usually with another clandestine seminarian. One day in April 1944, his partner, Jerzy Zachuta, didn't show up. After Mass, Karol ran to the Zachuta home to see what had happened; Jerzy had been arrested the night before and was shot a few days later. One was taken, another remained: "So many young people of my own age are losing their lives, *why not me*?"

On August 6, 1944, the Nazis swept the city, trying to arrest all its young men in order to forestall a possible repeat of the Warsaw Uprising, which had begun five days earlier. Karol hid in "The Catacomb" and received his orders: Sapieha was calling in all the clandestine seminarians. They would now live with the archbishop, underground and hidden, at the Metropolitan Curia. With the help of a friend's mother, Karol worked his way across town, dodging the German patrols, and disappeared into Franciszkańska 3, which would be his home until the following summer. The archbishop's drawing room was the dormitory for the underground seminary; other rooms in the residence became classrooms. Every day the seminarians could watch the elderly archbishop go into his chapel late at night to lay the day's problems and trials before the Lord.

Cardinal Sapieha ordained Karol Wojtyła to the priesthood in that chapel on November 1, 1946. Forty-five years later, I came to Poland to find out what caused the Revolution of 1989. Like all epic historical events, this singular revolution was a complex affair and I wasn't interested in one-size-fits-all explanations. I wanted to know when the Revolution of 1989 had been ignited. So I asked people, "When did this really get rolling?" And without exception, believers and unbelievers, Catholics and Jews, agnostics and atheists, conservatives, liberals, and radicals *all* said the same thing—it began during

Pope John Paul II's nine-day pilgrimage to Poland in June 1979. Which was one, powerful answer to the question the man who would become pope had asked himself in "The Catacomb": Why had he been spared? "*Why not me?*"

One year after Mehmet Ali Agca shot him down in his front yard, St. Peter's Square, Pope John Paul said that "in the designs of Providence, there are no mere coincidences." That's the truth about vocation, obedience, and abandonment that his remarkable story illustrates. Chance is for card games. God doesn't work that way.

---

What do the stories of Father Jerzy and young Karol Wojtyła have to do with you and your questions?

I hope it encourages you to think vocationally, rather than in terms of "career." A career is something you have, and if those ubiquitous "career planners" are right, you may have two, three, or four of them in a lifetime. It's much more important, though, to think about vocation. For *a vocation is something you are*.

I hope these two stories encourage you to find and get to know men and women who are living vocationally—husbands and wives, professionals and workers, priests and consecrated religious. Becoming a good person isn't just a matter of convincing yourself about certain moral truths, important as that is. It's also a matter of finding virtuous people and learning from them how to live like them. The same goes for vocation. You may not find people whose vocational dramas are quite so intense and public as Father Jerzy's or Pope John Paul's. That's fine. The drama is there to be discovered, if you look hard enough.

Being here in Poland, breathing the air of these remarkably ordinary places where extraordinary things happened, and thinking about how Poland has died and risen and died and risen again, should also help you understand a bit more about how history really works.

According to the conventional wisdom in the 1980s, Poland's communists had all the cards: they controlled politics, they controlled the economy, they controlled the army, and they controlled the media. The resistance Church in Poland—men like Father Jerzy, inspired by John Paul II—didn't believe that. With the Pope (who had learned this in underground resistance efforts like the Rhapsodic Theater), they were convinced that *culture is what drives history over the long haul.* A people in possession of its culture, a people that owns the truth about itself, has weapons of resistance that totalitarianism can't match. People determined to live the truth of who they are—people determined to live vocationally—are the most dynamic force in history.

This is, once again, countercultural Catholicism—at least in terms of how Western high culture thinks about how the world and history work. It's much more fashionable today to think of history as the product of economics, or politics, or some combination of politics-and-economics, than to think of history as the product of culture. But that's what this stop on our tour suggests—that "history" (which certainly includes politics and economics) is even more the product of friendship and love and commitment and faith and the great artifacts of literature and music and painting and sculpture to which those deepest yearnings of the human spirit give birth. For friendship and love and commitment and faith are the deepest aspirations of the human spirit. That's why, to return to an image I've used before, history is *His*-story, the story of

God at work in the world, often "underneath the surface of history," in a drama of salvation that *is* the human story, read in its proper depth.

Catholics can't think of history as flat. Catholics can't think of history as the exhaust fumes of the "means of production." Catholics can't think of history as politics, period. Catholics have a craggier view of the way things work. The world may consider it crankier, rather than craggier. Consider the possibility that it is, in fact, the far more humane view.

The obedience of faith has consequences for societies and for history, as well as individuals. The obedience of faith is profoundly countercultural. It's also, as we learn here, a difference that can make a lot of difference.

# 11

## The North American College Mausoleum, Campo Verano, Rome—The Hardest Questions

Every Roman knows Campo Verano, although it's a bit off the typical tourist track. Originally the estate of Lucius Verus, co-emperor with Marcus Aurelius from 161 to 169, Campo Verano was designated as Rome's municipal cemetery when Napoleon and his minions were running things Italian in the early nineteenth century. It took decades to build; the idea, a grandiose one, was that everyone who died in Rome would be buried there after it was opened on July 1, 1836. This being Italy, it took a while to complete the original plans—the great gates to the cemetery were only finished in 1878.

Campo Verano occupies an enormous tract of land, some three times the size of Vatican City, in the Tiburtino District near Stazione Termini, the main train station. The gated entrance is a good stone's throw from the Basilica of St. Lawrence Outside the Walls; Blessed Pius IX is buried there in a memorial chapel whose mosaics are well worth a look. Once you're a few hundred yards inside Campo Verano, you can't see the cemetery's boundaries in any direction.

As you walk past the flower vendors and through the entrance gates to begin exploring Campo Verano's various "neighborhoods," you quickly get the impression that the Italians handle death about the same way as they handle everything else—dramatically. Monuments, mausoleums, family tombs, and even individual grave sites vie for splendor and *bella figura*. There's a very mixed population here—a little past the entrance, you can look up a gravel path to the tomb of Garibaldi, a rabid anticlerical, off to the right (inappropriately enough, from an ideological point of view). Yet as you continue along a seeming infinity of paths, up and down hills and through small valleys, you'll also find squadrons of cardinals and other high-ranking clerics. According to one story, possibly apocryphal, students from Rome's Pontifical Gregorian University used to come here the night before exams to pray at the Gregorian faculty mausoleum—presumably to make sure that certain demanding professors stayed put. Politicians, movie stars, literary people, and ordinary Romans long forgotten to history are all here; you can actually get to know many of them from the photos or etchings that you find on their tombstones.

I first visited Campo Verano on All Souls' Day, November 2, 2001, when I went there with several faculty members and students from the Pontifical North American College for a memorial Mass at the college mausoleum. In the first half of the twentieth century, American seminarians who died in Rome were buried in this three-story stone building; the annual memorial Mass is a college tradition; and as I was staying at the college while working in Rome, I was invited to come along. After Mass, while exploring the inscriptions on the vaults inside the mausoleum, I came across the name *Franciscus Parater*. One of the seminarians asked whether I had read "Frank Parater's Prayer" in the college *Manual of Prayers*. I had to admit that I hadn't. "Don't miss it," was my young friend's advice.

Frank Parater had come to Rome in November 1919 to study for the priesthood as a candidate for the Diocese of Richmond. Twenty-two years old at the time, he was one of Richmond's most impressive young men in his day, a model student and exceptional Scout leader whose character and courtesy cut through the genteel anti-Catholicism of that time and place. He had first felt attracted to a monastic vocation and began his studies at Belmont Abbey Seminary College in North Carolina, with an eye to becoming a Benedictine. During his two years at Belmont Abbey, though, Frank Parater decided to dedicate himself to the diocesan priesthood in a more active ministry, despite his inclinations toward a more contemplative life.

A month after arriving in Rome, Frank Parater wrote the prayer to which my young friend at Campo Verano had referred: "An Act of Oblation to the Sacred Heart of Jesus." It was in fact a spiritual last will and testament, which Parater left in an envelope with instructions to open it only in the event of his death. In his prayer, he offered himself for the conversion of his beloved state:

> *I have nothing to leave or give but my life and this I have consecrated to the Sacred Heart to be used as He wills. I have offered my all for the conversion of non-Catholics in Virginia. This is what I live for and in case of death what I die for. . . . Since my childhood I have wanted to die for God and my neighbor. Shall I have this grace? I do not know, but if I go on living, I shall live for this same purpose; every action of my life here is offered for the spread and success of the Catholic Church in Virginia . . . I shall be of more service to my diocese in Heaven than I can ever be on earth.*

In late January 1920, after just two months in Rome, Frank Parater contracted rheumatism, which developed into rheumatic fever. On January 27 he was taken to a hospital run by the Blue Nuns, where he suffered intense pain for two weeks. When the college spiritual director came to the hospital to give him the Last Rites, Frank Parater wanted to get up from his deathbed to receive his last holy communion kneeling; the doctors wouldn't permit it, so he knelt on the bed to receive the Viaticum, the "food for the journey." The college rector offered the votive Mass of the Sacred Heart for Frank Parater on February 6. He died the next day. His prayer was found in his room when a fellow student was gathering up his belongings. Pope Benedict XV and Pope Pius XI both asked for copies of "Frank Parater's Prayer."

Then the world and the Church seemed to move on, although the few who remembered were convinced that Frank Parater was keeping an eye on the Diocese of Richmond from a distance, so to speak. It took another Richmond seminarian, studying in Rome in the 1970s, to bring the Frank Parater story back to life. Having become fascinated by this striking tale during his own studies, Father J. Scott Duarte kept the story in mind after his own ordination and during his graduate studies. Years of Father Duarte's patient research paid off in January 2002, when the Diocese of Richmond officially opened the cause for the beatification of The Servant of God Frank Parater, Seminarian. Thousands of Catholics around the United States are now linked to this cause through a great chain of prayer, asking Frank Parater's intercession for their needs and asking God to bless the cause for his beatification with a miracle.

---

Frank Parater's story isn't an Everyman story. He died very young; he died heroically, away from home; and in some sense he not only embraced his premature death but anticipated and welcomed it as the best gift he could make of his life. There aren't a lot of us who are going to die that way. Yet for all its singularity, Frank Parater's story is a powerful one, particularly for a generation that often finds commitment difficult. In any case, here we are at Campo Verano at Frank Parater's tomb, which is as good a place as any to think about two questions this young son of Virginia seemingly answered to his own satisfaction before he died eight months short of his twenty-third birthday: Is there any meaning in suffering? Is death the final absurdity?

Once upon a time, indeed as recently as the mid-twentieth century, those were assumed to be two of the enduring questions of the human condition. No longer. Advances in medicine, and the promise of even greater progress through the application of our new genetic knowledge to curing disease, have led some doctors, geneticists, and biotech engineers to speak quite bluntly about the immortality project—not merely ending suffering but making us virtually immortal, here on this earth.

All of which led my friend Cardinal Francis George of Chicago to a sobering observation a few years ago. "Do you realize," the cardinal asked me, "that we're going to spend the rest of our lives trying to convince people that suffering and death are good for you?" It's hard to imagine something that cuts more deeply against the grain of contemporary American culture, so absorbed as it is by the pleasure principle. Yet that's what Catholics are going to have to do. And the first step in convincing others is convincing ourselves.

---

Let's start with suffering.

The first thing to notice about suffering is that suffering is something that only human beings undergo. Dogs and cats and cows and sheep feel pain; only human beings suffer. That's because our suffering is not simply physical, but mental and spiritual. Physical suffering can, of course, lead to spiritual anguish. But we can suffer morally and spiritually without any physical pain, and the less tangible forms of suffering are often the worst. If you've ever had a broken arm or leg, you've known one kind of pain; if a friend has betrayed you, you've known another, and likely worse, pain. Love spurned, plans frustrated, the incomprehension of parents, the indifference or cruelty of teachers—these are forms of moral and spiritual suffering that wound more deeply and ache more sharply than broken bones.

That suggests that suffering is telling us something important about ourselves as human beings—*we have souls; the "me" that makes me a unique person isn't just a bundle of neurons.* Suffering is another of those human experiences that point us beyond the ordinary to its near far side, where we meet the extraordinary—which in this case means the human soul and its capacity for endurance, courage, and self-sacrifice. Suffering isn't just a problem; it's part of the mystery, the transcendence, of the human experience.

The second thing we might notice about suffering is that *suffering has something to do with freedom.* As you've doubtless found out, a lot of very bright people find it easier to reconcile suffering with a purpose-free universe than to reconcile suffering with the idea of a good God. And truth to tell, some conventional religious answers haven't been very helpful here. To say that God "permits" suffering, for example, seems to make God into a blundering fool or a sadist. The biblical answer to this quandary, which informs the Catholic answer, is to recognize that suffering, like evil, is one of the implications of freedom—at least as men and women have lived their freedom since the stories recorded in Genesis. God created a world of freedom because, among other things, God desires the love of men and women who freely choose to love him, as they freely choose to love one another. And a world of freedom is a world in which things often go wrong, with suffering as one result.

The third thing to be said about suffering, from a Catholic perspective, is this: at the bottom of the bottom line, *suffering isn't a problem to be "solved" but a mystery to be engaged, in love*. When the Church says that something is a "mystery," it doesn't mean "mystery" in the sense that solving a crime is figuring out a "mystery." Rather, by "mystery" the Church means some essential truth that can be grasped only in an act of love. We don't get the Catholic "answer" to the mystery of suffering by completing a syllogism; the Catholic "answer" to the mystery of suffering comes through an encounter with Jesus Christ.

God's creation of the world was a free act of divine love, a love that spilled out of the inner life of God himself. God's love, therefore, is what gives true meaning to whatever exists—including suffering. God gives his answer to the world's question about the meaning of suffering through a demonstration. The dramatic climax of the demonstration of God's love for the world, and the capacity of that love to give meaning to the most intense suffering, is the cross of Christ. On the cross, in the suffering of Christ, God cleared out "all the refuse of the world's sin by burning it in the fire of suffering love," as Hans Urs von Balthasar once put it.

When the Son takes all the world's evil and sin and suffering upon himself and offers it to the Father in a perfect act of obedience, and when God vindicates that act of radical obedience and love in the Resurrection, suffering itself is transformed. When Christ redeems us by his suffering, suffering itself is redeemed. The Christ who died for all offers a share in his redemption to all—and offers us the possibility that, by identifying our suffering with his, we, too, can participate in his redemptive suffering for the world. That's what Frank Parater knew, intuitively. When Christ made himself a sharer in human suffering, he enabled us to share in his redemption. When our suffering is identified with his, it becomes redemptive because it, like Christ's, is thereby linked to love. Offering our suffering for the good of others is sharing in the redeeming work of Christ. Offering our suffering for the good of others is one way we help the Church extend the saving work of Christ in history.

I had been taught these things in school, but it was years later when I saw the truth of redemptive suffering at work in a life. I had gotten to know Congressman Henry Hyde and his wife, Jeanne, over the years, and I visited, talked, and prayed with Jeanne in the hospital when she was being treated for cancer in the early 1990s. In her last illness, Jeanne Hyde offered her suffering for the great cause for which she and Henry had fought so long and nobly, and in doing so, it seemed to me, she was doing more good than she imagined. Who knew, I once wrote her, how many desperate, lonely young women had found the courage not to abort their children because of Jeanne's offering her suffering for their sakes? I was out of the country when Jeanne Hyde died. One of her sons told me a few weeks later that his mother's had been a peaceful, even happy death, because of her conviction that, in identifying her suffering with Christ's, she was somehow helping young women affirm the gift of life.

"No cross, no crown" is the maxim that sums up St. Paul's entire message in his second letter to those feisty and confused Corinthians—suffering prepares us for "an eternal weight of glory, beyond all comparison" (2 Corinthians 4:17). Transformed by the cross of Christ, our suffering is no longer an absurdity but rather another way to become the kind of people who can live with God forever. Suffering helps us learn to be comfortable in the blazing light of the God whose Son enters the world to suffer and die for it, and for us. Frank Parater knew that in his heart. So did Jeanne Hyde. That's why they died happily, ready for God.

All of which suggests that, for Catholics, suffering is a vocation. It's another way of making ourselves into the gifts for others that our own lives are to us. It's a way of growing into compassion—which, in its Latin root, means the capacity to "suffer with." Like the Good Samaritan, we learn through suffering, our own suffering and others', that you can't just "pass by" on the other side of the road of life. Suffering, our own and others', teaches us a fundamental human solidarity.

Like everything else in life, suffering looks different when we experience history as *His*-story—Christ's story—the story of redeeming love burning its way through the world. Peter Kreeft puts in nicely: when we look at history as *His*-story, suffering becomes the bass note "in a harmony whose high notes are lost in heaven." So don't think of suffering as spiritual castor oil. In the mystery of human life, suffering makes us the kind of people who can live in an eternity in which every tear has been wiped away, death is no more, and there is neither mourning nor crying nor pain (Revelation 21:1–5). Suffering makes us the kind of people who can live with Love itself, without suffering from it or getting bored by it.

---

You're going to live your Catholic life in a world in which death is increasingly seen as a disease to be cured. Hormonal therapies, the possibility of "replacement parts" being grown out of stem cells, and research into the genetic basis of aging all suggest the possibility that the human life span can be dramatically expanded, perhaps indefinitely. What does a "pro-life" Church say about that?

One of our wisest guides here in Leon Kass, whom President Bush appointed chairman of the President's Commission on Bioethics in 2001. Kass, a brilliant reader of both the Bible and the great books of the Western tradition, suggests that the immortality project has been built into modern science from its beginnings. Francis Bacon and René Descartes were quite open about the purpose of the new kind of experimental science they were launching in the seventeenth century—it was to "relieve man's estate," by which they meant nothing less than reversing Genesis and the sentence of death that has hung over every human being since Adam and Eve. That project now stands on the threshold of success. What should we think of that?

Kass, who's not arguing as a Catholic but as a man of reason, suggests that we should look at the immortality project with robust skepticism—not because it might not "work," in the technical sense, but because it would be lethal for humanity if it did work. Like Cardinal George, Leon Kass believes that death is good for us, in a deeply human if mysterious sense. In a brilliantly provocative article, "L'Chaim and Its Limits: Why Not Immortality?" Kass suggests that we reverse the question and ask, Is mortality a blessing? He then offers several reasons why the answer to that is emphatically yes.

Would an infinite life span (or even a life span extended twenty-five or fifty years) really increase our satisfaction? It's very unclear, he argues, that doing more of the same things for a much longer time, or even doing the occasional extraordinary things during a vastly expanded life span, would add to the sum total of human happiness. Then there's the question of human striving and what virtual immortality would do to that essential human quality: "Could life be serious or meaningful without the limit of mortality? Is not the limit on our time the ground of our taking life seriously and living it passionately?" When the Psalms enjoin us to "number our days" so that we may "get a heart of wisdom," the psalmist is teaching us a very large truth. Even pagans once understood this, Kass suggests. In the *Iliad* and the *Odyssey*, it's the immortals who are silly, frivolous, aimless; Homer's mortals, by comparison, are full of striving, passion, courage, and fellow-feeling.

Then, Kass reminds us, there are beauty and love. There is nothing beautiful, and there's no real love, in the brave new world—and that, in itself, is a warning. Then there's what Kass calls "the peculiarly human beauty of character," which brings us to the relationship between our mortality, on the one hand, and the virtues, on the other. Living life as the gift it is to us would be far more difficult without mortality, Kass proposes: "To be mortal means that it is possible to give one's life, not only in one moment, say, on the field of battle, but also in the many other ways in which we are able in action to rise above our attachment to survival"—or, I'd add, our attachment to our self-assertion, which is something we all cling to. Immortals, Kass argues, "cannot be noble." The only kind of people who can reach genuine nobility of character are those willing to spend "the precious coinage of the time of our lives for the sake of the noble and the good and the holy."

Yet, as Leon Kass frankly notes, "our soul's reach exceeds our grasp," and people will continue to seek an answer to the mystery of death. One answer is the immortality project. As Kass teaches us, though, that's an ultimately dehumanizing enterprise. "To argue that human life would be better without death," he writes, is "to argue that human life would be better off being something other than human." So what's the Catholic counterproposal? It's the Resurrection, and the eternal life with God that the Resurrection of Christ has made possible for us.

---

Kass suggests that what our souls really long for is not deathlessness but "wholeness, wisdom, goodness, and godliness—longings that cannot be satisfied fully in embodied earthly life." Catholics propose that these are precisely the longings that are satisfied in the resurrected, transfigured, and transformed life of the saints—those who have become the kind of people who can live with God forever. That's our Christian destiny *and our human destiny.* Kass has it exactly right when he argues, against the immortalists, that "mere continuance will not buy fulfillment." But transfiguration can. And transfiguration is what we are promised in the resurrection of the dead in the kingdom of God.

And it won't be the bore that "immortal life" here would almost certainly be. Perhaps without intending to, Leon Kass himself supplies the answer to why heaven won't be boring when he reminds us that "some activities . . . [may not] require finitude as a spur." The quest for understanding is one; we can imagine it continuing without the prod of mortality, for there is always something more to understand, to grasp more deeply. Friendship and love are two others; they seem capable of growing infinitely. *And that is exactly what awaits us in the kingdom of God:* an eternity of unfolding understanding and friendship and love.

There's one more reason—the most urgent one—why Catholics think that death is good for us: our dying gives us the opportunity to configure our lives most radically to the life of Christ. It's not just a question of a final deathbed offering-of-self in union with Christ, although when we pray for a "good death" that's what we're praying for. Our dying is something that should live in us every day, not morbidly but as part of our prayer. Knowing that we are to die—even if that death is, on the odds, far down the road—we should ask every day that our dying in small things, just as our dying to this life, will be configured to the sacrifice of Christ, which redeems all suffering and death.

Our old friend G. K. Chesterton once said that, while man has always lost his way, "modern man has lost his address." That address is the kingdom of God. Knowing it gives us directions for navigating the roads of this life, and gives our travel along those roads its ultimate human meaning.

---

Before we leave Campo Verano, let's think for a moment about another form of suffering and death—martyrdom.

Too many Catholics think of "martyrdom" as something that happened eighteen or nineteen hundred years ago (the classic cinematic image is Richard Burton, spurning the mad Caligula and walking hand in hand to death with Jean Simmons at the end of *The Robe*). In fact, though, we've just come through the greatest period of martyrdom in Christian history. During the Great Jubilee of 2000, a comprehensive study of twentieth-century martyrs was done and the results were striking—more Christians gave their lives for Christ in the twentieth century than in the previous nineteen centuries of Christian history combined. The Nazis and the communists spilled more Christian blood than Nero and Diocletian imagined possible.

That tells us something important about our times—or, perhaps better, the times of your parents and grandparents, which created the world for which you'll have to take responsibility. It tells us that hundreds of thousands of souls stood firm during the bloodiest century in the history of the world. As in the past, the light shone in the darkness and the darkness was not able to blot it out. Courage is possible; conviction is possible; commitment is possible. These are not just noble ideals. They're living realities. The modern martyrs teach us that.

They also teach us that the Church, for all its sinfulness and weakness, is still capable of nurturing great souls. As you probably know, the Catholic Church in Germany is in bad shape; there are more people at Mass in my suburban Washington parish at 8:00 A.M. on a Wednesday morning than I found in the Munich Cathedral at a Sunday Mass. Yet the German Church is fabulously rich (because of tax support) and many of its leaders still think of German Catholicism as the intellectual cutting edge of the world Church. It's all very strange, and more than a little odd. In late 2001 I was talking with Cardinal Joachim Meisner of Cologne about these problems and I asked him, "Your Eminence, what's the one thing German Catholicism will take from the twentieth century that's most important for the German Church in the twenty-first century?" Without hesitating an instant, the cardinal replied, "The eight hundred names in our Book of Martyrs."

He didn't mention the Church's financial resources; he didn't mention the German Church's extensive links to the Third World (in any given year, German Catholic development agencies give more aid to the Church in the developing world than the global budget of the U.S. Agency for International Development); he didn't cite German scholarship, the hundreds of German theologians, the great tradition of German biblical studies. He said, forcefully, "The eight hundred names in our Book of Martyrs." The witness of the men and women who had kept the light shining in the darkness of Nazi and communist paganism—that's what would revivify German Catholicism in the twenty-first century, the cardinal suggested. Given the ancient maxim that "the blood of martyrs is the seed of the Church," I think he may well be right. Who are young Germans going to look to for religious inspiration? Intellectuals, who are far more at ease telling you what they don't believe than what they do? Or martyrs?

Why has martyrdom has always been considered the highest form of Christian witness? I think it's because of that Law of the Gift we've discussed before. If a law of self-giving is hard-wired into us as the very structure of our spiritual and moral lives, then the most radical form of self-giving, of liberating obedience to that law, is the giving that is literally "unto death." The martyr is the Christian most fully conformed to the crucified Christ. The martyr is also the Christian witness who can, in his or her death, make the most radical, complete gift of self.

You're not likely to be called to martyrdom in the strict sense of the term. But the martyrs teach us something else—that death-to-self *is* the ultimate form of human liberation. And that kind of dying is something we can, and should, indeed must, do every day.

Suffering and death are good for us. As strange as that sounds, it's true.

12

# Chartres Cathedral, France—What Beauty Teaches Us

In an earlier letter, I recklessly suggested that the Sistine Chapel is the most extraordinary room in the world. Let me crawl out even farther on the comparative limb and propose that Chartres Cathedral is the most extraordinary building in the world. I've been in the Dome of the Rock in Jerusalem; it's magnificent, but it isn't Chartres. I've not been to the Taj Mahal, but I doubt that it could rival Chartres—stone and glass into which have been poured the obedience of faith and a passionate, transforming love for Christ, Mary, the world, and the beauty of the human. The result in what its builders imagined it to be—an antechamber to heaven.

It's a good thing to come here when you're young. I was forty-six, alas, before I first got to Chartres, with the help of my friend Jean Duchesne. Jean had been deeply involved in preparations for the 1997 World Youth Day in Paris, during which I stayed with his family in their Parisian flat. After a busy week, we all went to the Duchesnes' country place in Normandy to rest, and from there Jean and I drove to Chartres for the day. After a fine ramble through the French countryside, we glimpsed it on the near horizon without much warning: a great stone ship, massive yet ethereal, silhouetted against the sky. Imagine how a medieval pilgrim must have felt after days of trudging the dirt roads and pre-harvest fields of France when that vision came into sight.

The contemplative is not my natural cast of mind. But there was something about the cathedral of Chartres that rendered me, quite literally, speechless. Looking through and studying a great building for the first time, I usually like to talk about it with friends or a knowledgeable guide. Not here. Here, I just wanted to look, and admire, and absorb. Absorb what? It's not easy to say. Perhaps I'll simply call it the beauty of the place—the beauty of Chartres' stained glass. I didn't want to talk about it; I simply wanted to let the luminous splendors of that incomparable glass wash over me in great waves. I had the sense of praying, without words. Like the eleventh and twelfth stations of the Church of the Holy Sepulcher in Jerusalem, although for very different reasons, Chartres invites us to "practice the presence"—to rest and just *be*, in the beautiful, turbulent, peaceful presence of God.

Which is what I did for the better part of three hours, before my practical French friend suggested that it was time for lunch.

---

While we were eating, we talked about the Gothic and its peculiarities. You've read about the ways in which the vaulting, the height, and the flying buttresses of Gothic cathedrals evoke a sense of transcendence. So, obviously, do those extraordinary glass "walls" framed by intricately chiseled stone. The Gothic creates a sense of being suspended, of floating in space about itself; and when we're "inside" the Gothic we experience a similar sense of weightlessness. But all that's familiar to you. My friend Duchesne suggested a few other reasons for the Gothic's unique permeability to the transcendent.

Jean pointed out that Gothic is a particularly successful form of Christian architecture because it's cranky. Things aren't uniform. Chartres, for example, displays a settled determination *not* to be uniform. The great towers don't match—one is intricately decorated with stone webbing; the other is plainly roofed. Then there are those three great rose windows. Each is structured by a different geometric form, with circles dominating the south rose window, squares the north rose, and circles within asymmetrical ellipses the west rose. This jumble, Jean suggested, was quite deliberate: God didn't make a one-size-fits-all world, and the builders of Chartres wanted that to be reflected in their design.

The Gothic also manages to combine the majestic and the personal in ways that other styles don't quite match. The majesty of Chartres is obvious; you have to look a little more closely for the personal, but it's there. For the people who made Chartres possible by their generosity—its donors large and small—are recognized in that extraordinary glass. Plowmen, priests, nobles, drapers, bakers, butchers, bankers, fishmongers, vintners, farriers, apothecaries, haberdashers, wheelwrights, carpenters, shoemakers, and pilgrims all contributed to the building of Chartres. They're all memorialized, not by name but by luminous image in over a hundred scenes scattered throughout the windows. Some of them gave fortunes; others undoubtedly gave little more than the biblical widow's mite. They're all there, and they all count, in the democracy of receiving-and-giving that is the Church.

Which is appropriate enough, because the building of Chartres, which certainly involved enormous skill and craftsmanship, was also something of a populist enterprise. Today's Gothic masterpiece was built out from an earlier structure that had been badly damaged in a fire which destroyed much of the city and left only the crypt, the tower foundations, and the west facade of the twelfth-century cathedral. Once it was known that the town's most famous relic—the Sancta Camisia, a garment believed to have been worn by Mary when she gave birth to Christ—had been spared, the people immediately demanded that a new cathedral be built. Thousands of townspeople went voluntarily to the quarry at Berchères, singing hymns and chanting. They loaded wooden-wheeled carts with great blocks of stone and pushed, pulled, and dragged the load five miles back to Chartres, singing and chanting all the way.

The entire Chartres project was accompanied by an exceptional outpouring of generosity. The great fire occurred in 1194. By 1223, less than thirty years later, much of the structure we know today had been completed, thanks to the philanthropy of the donors and the enthusiasm of the builders and craftsmen. The Cathedral of the Assumption of Our Lady wasn't consecrated until 1260 (at which point the idea of building nine steeples was, happily, abandoned). But the bulk of the work had been done in a breathtakingly short period of time, in a world without electricity or steam engines or gigantic cranes of the sort you now see at every major building site in the world.

Why? I think there were several reasons, and they're all interesting. The Sancta Camisia was a famous relic that attracted large numbers of pilgrims. The local people thought of its home, the Chartres cathedral, as "the earthly palace of the Queen of Heaven," according to the great Chartres scholar and guide Malcolm Miller. And if the queen's home burned down, her loyal subjects ought to build her another home, even more splendid than the last. That was certainly one driving force behind the rapid construction of Chartres.

Then there was the sense of expectation that permeated medieval life. The people of the Middle Ages took the idea of Christ's Second Coming very seriously. But the Lord himself had said, "Of that day and hour no one knows, not even the angels in heaven, nor the Son, but the Father only" (Matthew 24:36). So it was best to be prepared—and by "prepared," medievals meant more than attending to their own souls. They meant preparing places appropriately glorious to welcome Christ's return. You can't really understand the fantastic burst of creativity that resulted in the great Gothic cathedrals without wrestling with that fact: people were quite convinced that they were preparing a guest room, so to speak, for Christ himself. That was a powerful spur to energy, creativity, and generosity.

Those convictions also explain why the world-famous glass of Chartres is organized the way it is. You've probably been told that Gothic stained glass is didactic, its images intended to teach the basics of the biblical story and Christian faith to illiterates. That's true as far as it goes, but to appreciate the imaginative genius involved in a place like Chartres means widening the lens of our understanding a bit. For the men who designed the Chartres windows, and the master craftsmen who executed those designs, intended the cathedral's glass walls to be nothing less than a comprehensive account of salvation history—the world's story read as *His*-story, to return to an image I've used before. That intention neatly coincided with the didactic purpose of the windows: What would be a more fitting reception room for the returning and glorified Christ than one that told the whole story that had brought the world to this climactic point—recognizing and welcoming its redeemer?

That's why the first stunning quartet of windows over the royal portal to the cathedral, the west rose and its three accompanying lancets, are a summary of the great narrative that unfolds throughout the rest of Chartres cathedral. The central and largest window in the triptych of lancets is the Incarnation window—central because it depicts the chief dynamic of history: God's love for the world, manifest in God's Son come in the flesh for the world's salvation. The left lancet is the window of the Passion and Resurrection, equally stunning in its evocation of the central act in the drama of redemption. The west rose itself is dedicated to the Last Judgment—the climax of history as *His*-story. It's the right lancet below the west rose that perhaps best expresses the richness of medieval faith and imagination, however, through the use of a favorite medieval image—the Jesse Tree. Let me give you a brief excerpt from Malcolm Miller's description of it:

> *Jesse, the father of David, reclines at the bottom of the window upon a bed of white linen. He is wrapped in a bright red, yellow-bordered blanket . . . His feet are*

> *bare, like those of prophets and evangelists . . . Above him a lamp hangs on a golden chain and a curtain flutters from a red semicircular arch, beyond which, in the spandrels, spreads the royal city of David, Bethlehem.*
>
> *From Jesse's groin, the source of life, springs not a rod, but the trunk of a tree, in the center of which the sap can be clearly seen rising through a succession of four kings of Judah, richly clad in red and green, yellow and purple, against a background of intense blue. . . . Although they carry neither attribute nor inscription, the four crowned figures probably represent David, Solomon, Roboam* [sic], *and Abia, the first in Matthew's long list of twice-fourteen kings of Judah, Christ's royal ancestors . . .*
>
> *Christ is seated at the summit of the tree . . . surrounded by doves that symbolize the seven gifts of the Holy Spirit . . . Contained within red half-circles on either side of the figures in the tree, and turned towards them, are twice seven Old Testament prophets bearing scrolls on which their names are written . . . Thus Christ's spiritual forebears frame His ancestors of the flesh and prepare for the narrative of the Incarnation, the temporal fulfillment of the prophecies, in the adjacent central lancet window.*

Chartres is inconceivable without the obedience of faith. The people who built Chartres thought that they were building an earthly representation of the New Jerusalem—but perhaps "representation" isn't quite the right word. Those who built Chartres and those who gave of their substance to make Chartres possible believed that they were in the antechamber of heaven in this place. Chartres is a uniquely permeable "border" between the mundane and the transcendent, the visible and the invisible, the ordinary and the extraordinary, the human and the divine: *and that's exactly what it was meant to be*. That's why Chartres has the awe-inspiring effect it has. That's why Chartres renders us speechless. To pass through the royal portal into this privileged space is, in Malcolm Miller's words, as if one were passing "through the gates of Paradise into the heavenly city itself, with its walls opened and set with glittering jewel-like stained glass windows which diffuse a mystic and divine essence: light."

Chartres is both a powerful expression and a powerful confirmation of the Catholic sacramental imagination. Here is where you can experience, through brilliantly luminous color, the permeability of this world to the really real world.

---

The experience of Chartres' incomparable beauty is our primary reason for coming here. At the same time, as you fix this beauty in your mind's eye, let me suggest that there are some things to be learned here—things that are important for your Catholic life.

Chartres powerfully reinforces our old friend Chesterton's claim that tradition is the democracy of the dead. Do we want to give the people who built Chartres "votes" in the forming of our humanity and our faith today? I certainly hope so. To cut ourselves off from the civilization that produced something as beautiful as this is to lobotomize ourselves culturally. When I was a boy, intellectually assertive Catholic youngsters were urged to read a book with the in-your-face title, *The Thirteenth—Greatest of Centuries*. It's not an argument I'm all that eager to defend, particularly as I'd prefer a thirteenth (or any other) century that included modern dentistry, indoor plumbing, antibiotics, and anesthesia. But that kind of unapologetic medievalism raises a point you ought to consider—and that's whether the Middle Ages have gotten a bad rap that's doing damage to us, and to the human project, here and now.

"Medieval" has become an all-purpose put-down in American high culture, a synonym for "obscurantist," "undemocratic," "primitive," "unenlightened." That's a *very* hard case to sell here at Chartres, though. There's nothing obscurantist about a human artifact that uses light to create powerful visual and emotional experiences of transcendence; far from being "obscurantist," the medieval world as embodied by Chartres cathedral is almost blindingly luminous. As for "undemocratic," look at all those workers and tradesmen memorialized in the donor windows—there's a lot more democratic sensibility here than in, say, early American Protestant churches with their class-stratified pew rents and balconies reserved for servants and slaves.

Primitive? Quite the opposite. The unity of design and the iconographic integrity of Chartres speak to us of people with a coherent and rationally defensible idea of who they were, what the world was, and how things fit together. That's rather different from the contemporary university world, where very few of the best and brightest are prepared to claim that *anything* is "true"—and thus end up believing the most preposterous things about what makes for human happiness. (Remember your Chesterton again: people who have stopped believing in God don't believe nothing; they believe anything.)

"Unenlightened"? This is a place built of and for light and enlightenment. Chartres' resolute insistence on the Catholic "both/and"—visible *and* invisible, nature *and* grace, material *and* transcendent—seems ever so much more human and humane, so much more enlightened and enlightening, than the flat, windowless, locked-down world of the modern secular materialist.

So if coming to Chartres teaches you what Mr. Jefferson would have called a "decent respect," in this case for the rich human and spiritual experience of the medieval world, it's been worth the journey.

Chartres also teaches us about the importance of beauty and the beautiful for Catholic faith. The sad fact is that a lot of contemporary Catholicism is ugly: ugly buildings, ugly furnishings, ugly decorations, ugly vestments, ugly music. There are exceptions, huge exceptions, to be sure. But the general Catholic drift in the United States is not, to put it gently, toward the beautiful. That's not just an aesthetic problem. It's a serious religious and theological problem.

Why? Because beauty helps prepare us to be the kind of people who can be comfortable in heaven—the kind of people who can live with God forever. Beautiful things and beautiful music draw us out of ourselves and into an encounter with a truth that's beyond us, yet accessible to our senses. I've talked a lot in these letters about self-giving, not self-assertion, as the royal road to human happiness and spiritual growth. Well, there are few greater obstacles to self-giving than self-absorption.

And the beauty that, by its very nature, draws us out of ourselves is an antidote to self-absorption. The beauty of Beatrice drew Dante out of himself and into paradise, and into an encounter with the beauty that is Love itself. The same experience is available to us in our encounters with the beautiful.

The joy of beauty is another anticipation of the kingdom, and another way that we're prepared for the kingdom. How are we to become the kind of people who can be happy forever—especially those of us who are congenitally grouchy? Beauty, by giving us experiences of unalloyed joy here and now, prepares us for that dimension of life with God. So does beauty's inexhaustibility—the fact that we never tire of a beautiful painting, sculpture, building, poem, or piece of music. In my last letter I spoke of friendship and the quest for understanding as human realities that we could imagine "growing" indefinitely, even infinitely. The same applies to the inexhaustibility of beauty, which is another reason why beauty prepares us for, even as it anticipates, life in the kingdom, life with God forever. As Hans Urs von Balthasar once wrote, the more we know and love and understand a great work of art, the more we recognize that we can't, in the final analysis, "grasp" its genius. That's why we never "outgrow" a beloved work of art. And that inexhaustibility prepares us to "contemplate God in the beatific vision, [when] we will *see* that God is forever the ever-greater."

So beauty helps deepen in us a sense of our human and spiritual destiny, which is life forever in the light and love of the Holy Trinity. Beauty has one other link to faith that I'd like to mention briefly.

Beauty is something that even the most skeptical moderns can *know*. Balthasar once wrote that people who doubt they can say what's good or what's true can't be similarly skeptical about the meaning of beauty, once they've experienced it. People *know* that they *know* what's beautiful. Thus beauty is one way we can introduce our doubting friends and colleagues to the mystery they often deny: the mystery that *there is truth and we can know it*. Once they've crossed the bridge of radical skepticism, the results can be dramatic and surprising. You'll remember Father Jay Scott Newman from an earlier letter. It's worth noting that the Gothic beauty of the Princeton chapel played a considerable role in breaking him free of the rationalistic atheism he had adopted as a teenager and bringing him to Christ.

---

All of which takes us back to the great theological mentor of the Middle Ages, St. Augustine, and his *Confessions*. In perhaps the most famous and lyrical moment in this first true autobiography, Augustine takes himself to task for his resistance and then exults in his surrender to the God who is Beauty itself:

> *Late have I loved thee, O Beauty ever ancient, ever new, late have I loved thee! You were within, but I was outside, and it was there that I searched for you. In my unloveliness I plunged into the lovely things which you created. You were with me, but I was not with you. Created things kept me from you; yet if they had not been in you they would not have been at all. You called, you shouted, and you broke*

> *through my deafness. You flashed, you shone, and you dispelled my blindness. You breathed your fragrance over me; I drew in my breath and now I pant for you. I have tasted you, and now I hunger and thirst for more. You touched me, and I burned for your embrace.*

The Catholic spirit can't live without beauty; the *human* spirit can't live without beauty. Sometime when you're in Florence, I hope you'll go to the Convent of San Marco. As you come up the stairway, you'll find yourself looking down, as we all do when climbing stairs; then, at the top, you'll look up and suddenly be confronted with the gossamer beauty of Fra Angelico's famous fresco of the Annunciation. But that's not the only thing to be pondered in San Marco. Several dozen cells—the Dominicans' modest rooms—have been restored and preserved, from the days when Girolamo Savonarola ruled the community. The cells are small, there is (obviously) no indoor plumbing, and you can imagine the austerity in which these Dominicans lived, even without the prod of Savonarola's passion for penitence. Then you notice something else. Each of these plain cells, utterly lacking in what we imagine as creature comforts, has a small Fra Angelico fresco in it—a biblical scene from the life of Christ or the life of Mary. From the prior to the humblest monk, *everyone* had a beautiful Fra Angelico fresco in his cell. Because everyone needs beauty. We need it for our souls. We need beauty to prepare our souls, and the rest of us, for what lies ahead, when we come home at last.

The builders of Chartres knew that. The prior who commissioned Fra Angelico to fresco a small portion of every single friar's cell knew that. We should know it today.

---

Let me close this letter by pulling a few of the threads of our conversation together, through an observation about icons. Icons have always been an integral part of the piety of the eastern Catholic Churches—local churches with a Byzantine liturgy that have remained in full communion with Rome. Icons have not been a significant part of the Catholic Church of the West, however, until recently. Now many parish churches display icons, and icons are readily available in Catholic bookstores and religious goods shops. An increasing number of Catholics pray with icons in their homes. Why?

In part, I suspect, because of a reaction to the not infrequent ugliness I have already mentioned. Even the most sterile cinder block "worship space" (another of those awful AmChurch neologisms) is ennobled by an icon. Post–Vatican II Catholics may be discovering the power of icons after too many preconciliar decades of religious "art" that was, truth to tell, shlock. But whether it's in response to modern AmChurch ugliness or old-fashioned Catholic bad taste, the new interest in icons is instructive for the same reason that Chartres is instructive—it tells us that beauty and prayer go together.

When Chartres invites us out of ourselves into a realm of luminous beauty, it's inviting us, however gently, to pray. The brilliant craftsmen who put those extraordinary blues and reds into the glass of Chartres intended their work as an offering to the Queen of Heaven, patroness and protector of their city. At the same time, the glass they made was an invitation to a wider and deeper vision of the human estate, a vision that necessarily leads to praise and thanksgiving, intercession and contrition—in a word, to prayer. The same is true of icons. I think that's what so many people who now buy icons or applaud the erection of icons in their churches intuitively understand.

As we've discussed before, we don't merely look *at* icons; we look *through* them and discover ourselves engaged with the Truth the iconographer has written. We meet the truth of Christ through the Christos Pantokrator, as we meet the truth of Mary in the Black Madonna and the truth of the Trinity in Rublev's famous evocation of the angels' visitation to Abraham. All of these encounters are invitations to prayer. Beauty is an invitation to pray. The God who is Augustine's "Beauty ever ancient, ever new" pours beauty into the world as one facet of his thirst for us. God asks us to drink at the wellspring of beauty here and now in order to drink, finally, of his own ineffable and inexpressible and inexhaustible beauty in the New Jerusalem.

Through the beauty of Chartres we encounter what the early Greek Fathers of the Church called the "divinization" of man. Cardinal Christoph Schönborn, O.P., the archbishop of Vienna, reminds us that this "divinization" of man is made possible by what the cardinal calls "the *humanization* of God"—the Incarnation. When God enters history in the flesh, history isn't the only thing radically transformed; so are the possibilities of the human. Through the Incarnation, human nature is led to its fulfillment, its completion.

That's the truth shining through the ineffable blues of the Chartres windows. That's the truth that makes every icon possible. That is grace at work—God's outpouring of his superabundant life into the world and into our lives. Like Augustine, we burn for the embrace of the Beauty that is always the same and always new. That burning, which God himself has built into us, is the beginning of every prayer.

13

# The Old Cathedral, Baltimore—Freedom for Excellence

Baltimore is home to the most historic Catholic building in the United States. It goes today by the ungainly title of the Basilica of the National Shrine of the Assumption of the Blessed Virgin Mary. For Baltimoreans of my generation, though, it is, was, and always will be "the Old Cathedral." Architectural critics and historians will confirm what seems clear as you look at the Old Cathedral from the corner of Cathedral and Mulberry Streets—this is one of the finest pieces of Federal period architecture in America. That will become even more apparent when a long overdue restoration is completed in 2006. The man who built America's first Catholic cathedral intended it to be a living metaphor—for Catholicism and America, for Catholicism and democracy, for Catholicism and religious freedom. We can visit his tomb in the Old Cathedral crypt at the back of the building.

John Carroll, the first and arguably the greatest of Catholic bishops in the United States, was born in Upper Marlborough, a small hamlet in southern Maryland, in 1735. His mother's family, the Darnalls, were related to the founder of the colony, Lord Baltimore, who had established "Maryland" as a place of religious freedom for his English fellow Catholics in 1634; his father's people, the Carrolls, produced generation after generation of distinguished personalities, including John Carroll's cousin, Charles Carroll of Carrollton, last surviving signer of the Declaration of Independence. John Carroll joined the Jesuits, was educated in France, and began his priestly work in Europe. After the Jesuits were suppressed by Pope Clement XIV in 1773, Father Carroll returned to Maryland and lived with his mother in what is now suburban Washington, D.C. When the American Revolution got going in earnest, Father Carroll was recruited to the patriot cause, joining his cousin Charles, Benjamin Franklin, and Samuel Chase on a fruitless mission to Canada to persuade the colonists there to join the revolt against Great Britain. On the way back home, Franklin fell gravely ill and Father Carroll nursed him back to health; the two remained friends for the rest of their lives.

After the success of the Revolution, Father Carroll began organizing the few priests in the new country (there were scarcely more than two dozen). The Holy See named Carroll "head of the missions in the provinces . . . of the United States" in 1784, and for the next five years Carroll traveled to Catholic communities up and down the eastern seaboard, reported to Rome on this unprecedented situation of a free Church in a free society, and defended Catholics against attacks from the bigots of the day. In 1789 Pope Pius VI confirmed the choice of the American clergy and appointed John Carroll first bishop of the Diocese of Baltimore—which was to cover the entire country. Thus John Carroll became the *only* Catholic bishop between the Atlantic and the Mississippi, and between Canada and Florida, not just the first Catholic bishop in the United States. Bishop Carroll became Archbishop Carroll in 1808, when his vast diocese was divided and new sees were erected in Boston, New York, Philadelphia, and Bardstown (Kentucky). He had cordial relations with the political leaders of his time, including George Washington and Thomas Jefferson. His episcopal headaches and heartaches came from a cantankerous clergy and from laymen who, accustomed to managing their own affairs, demanded proprietary control over their churches, too; the more ornery of the latter took their bishop to court, where he was consistently vindicated.

In the story of the Catholic Church in the United States, the adjective "first" is more often applied to John Carroll than to any other figure: first superior of the "American mission"; first bishop and first archbishop; founder of the first seminary (St. Mary's) and the first college (Georgetown); protector of Saint Elizabeth Seton and thus a founding father of the Catholic school system; the first bishop to ordain a priest in the United States; the first bishop to ordain other bishops in the United States; and, to come down to cases, the builder of the first cathedral. Archbishop Carroll had a very specific idea in mind for his cathedral—it was to embody the Catholic commitment to American democracy, and specifically to the religious freedom enshrined in the First Amendment to the Constitution. That dictated a distinctively American style of architecture—a distinctively American adaptation of classical forms. So Carroll employed Benjamin Henry Latrobe, who would also do important work on the U.S. Capitol, as his architect.

Latrobe's genius produced a building that is, at one and the same time, distinctively American *and* visibly linked to the Christian past. The most innovative feature in the Baltimore cathedral was a double-dome system, whose technical specifications Latrobe seems to have discussed with Thomas Jefferson. The great outer dome of the Baltimore Cathedral had twenty-four large skylights; the inner dome gathered the natural light from the skylights and filtered it through a single large oculus into the interior of the cathedral. Latrobe's double-dome system is now being restored, and in 2006 (the bicentenary of John Carroll's cornerstone ceremony) you'll be able to see the Baltimore Cathedral as Latrobe and Carroll imagined it—bathed in a diffused light suggesting both freedom and transcendence.

That's John Carroll's tomb, nearest you on the lower level of the left side of the Old Cathedral crypt. Seven other archbishops of Baltimore are buried here. Directly across from Carroll is James Cardinal Gibbons, a Baltimore native, second U.S. cardinal, and the most prominent Catholic personality in the United States for some forty years, from the last two decades of the nineteenth century through the first two decades of the twentieth. His book, *The Faith of Our Fathers*, was an exceptionally successful piece of apologetics when it was first published in 1876, and it's still in print today. Above Carroll rests Martin John Spalding, who came from Louisville to Baltimore (a city of Southern sympathies occupied by Union troops) during the Civil War. Spalding hailed from another venerable Maryland family, and his leadership at the Second Plenary Council of Baltimore in 1867, like Gibbons's at the Third Plenary Council in 1884, helped set the pattern of Catholic life in the United States for decades. Had he not died prematurely,

Spalding would almost certainly have been the first American cardinal. Next to Spalding is his predecessor, Francis Kenrick, who translated the entire Bible into English (his tempestuous brother Peter, archbishop of St. Louis, opposed the U.S. bishops' sponsorship of his brother's translation of the Bible and left Rome rather than vote for or against the decree on papal infallibility at Vatican I). Next to Gibbons is his successor, Michael Curley, a blunt, no-nonsense Irishman who raised eyebrows in Baltimore's more refined parlors but who was loved by the poor, the black, and the elderly—and who died utterly destitute in 1947, believing that no bishop should ever leave worldly goods behind him.

It's an extraordinary array of personalities and it's fitting that they should be here, because this cathedral is where they and their fellow bishops solemnized many of their most important decisions. The seven "provincial councils" and three "plenary councils" of Baltimore, which involved all the bishops of the United States, were the largest legislative assemblies of Catholic bishops between the sixteenth-century Council of Trent and the First Vatican Council (1869–1870). The Baltimore councils, whose most solemn moments were always celebrated in Carroll's cathedral, devised the U.S. parish system, mandated Catholic schools in those parishes, regulated the sacramental life of the Church, authorized the famous *Baltimore Catechism*, defended Catholicism against the frequent attacks of anti-Catholic bigots, launched the Catholic University of America, and dealt with issues ranging from appropriate dress for the clergy to the laws of fasting and abstinence. Until the Second Vatican Council dramatically changed the face of the Catholic Church in the United States, it's fair to say that the distinctively Catholic way of being American and the distinctively American way of being Catholic were defined here, in this building, by those councils. Here all the developments taking place throughout the country were distilled, and future plans laid, by the bishops of the United States.

As I mentioned in my first letter, I got acquainted with this great building when, at six and a half years old, I came to the Old Cathedral School, then at 7 West Mulberry Street, in September 1957. I made my first holy communion in the Old Cathedral on May 3, 1959. I graduated from college in the Old Cathedral on May 20, 1973. My son, Stephen, was baptized here on January 31, 1988. In recent years, I've tried to help the project to restore the Old Cathedral to Latrobe's original design, which promises it a third century of vigorous life. But I haven't brought you here for a walk down nostalgia lane—although if you like, I can show you the precise pew where Tommy Ostendorf, standing beside me in an identical white suit with white short pants and white socks, sang "Oh, Small White Host" off-key on May 3, 1959. Rather, I'd like to think out loud with you here about the relationship between Catholicism and democracy. There's no more fitting place to do that in the United States—which also makes this a good place to think about the meaning of freedom.

---

Catholics have, or should have, a different "story" about the origins of modern Western democracy than the "story" on tap in most schools today—the story that is refracted into our politics, our courts, and the media. According to this conventional story line, "democracy" is, by and large, a product of the Enlightenment—of

Hobbes and Locke and the Glorious Revolution of 1688, which finally subordinated royal willfulness to Parliament. "Democracy," on this understanding, required the overthrow of centuries of medieval obscurantism and royal absolutism (both typically identified with the Catholic Church). Vindicated in such contemporary dramas as the American civil rights movement and the Revolution of 1989 in east central Europe, democracy is now well established wherever the institutions of democratic governance (legislatures, an independent judiciary, an accountable executive, a free press, free and open elections, etc.) flourish. That's the conventional story.

There's another, and better, way to think about the story of democracy.

A Catholic reading of this history would suggest that you'll find deeper, sturdier roots of democracy in those often scorned Middle Ages. It's true that democracy had to supplant absolutism in Europe; it's also true that absolutism was an aberration in European history, not a natural evolution from the medieval world. The Middle Ages weren't "absolutist" in any sense of the term. On the contrary, the Middle Ages were a time of robust social pluralism. Associational life flourished in the Middle Ages, through institutions like the guilds you saw memorialized in the stained glass of Chartres. Those institutions and the medieval Church (including the papacy) were powerful checks on the absolutist pretensions of kings. Royal absolutism wasn't a feature of Catholic Christendom; absolutist political tendencies got the bit in their teeth after Christendom fractured in the Reformation.

The Catholicism of the Middle Ages nourished and supported independent, voluntary associations—religious communities, guilds, fraternal societies, charitable organizations. In the medieval view of things (unlike some Enlightenment-influenced views), there's more to society than the individual and the state. There's what the anticommunist dissidents who made the Revolution of 1989 called "civil society," which almost everyone now recognizes is a prerequisite for a stable, effective democracy. The medieval Catholic world lived "civil society" without ever defining it as such.

Catholicism did more than support the social institutions and way of life that eventually helped make democracy possible, however. The Catholic Church *taught* European man—taught him ideas and values that would later prove crucial to the success of the democratic project in the modern world.

For instance?

When Abraham Lincoln, in his *Gettysburg Address*, referred to a national rebirth of freedom "under God," he was unintentionally adverting to the most fundamental idea that Western civilization learned from Catholicism: that God's sovereignty transcends and stands in judgment on all worldly sovereignties. Because God is God, Caesar is not God and neither are Caesar's successors, be they kings, presidents, prime ministers, or party general secretaries. And because Caesar and his successors aren't God, their power is limited, not absolute; in addition to Caesar's legitimate power, there are other legitimate powers in the world.

So the state *cannot* be all there is. Long before Enlightenment political theorists began challenging royal absolutism with ideas like Montesquieu's "separation of powers," Western civilization learned the idea of "limited government" in the school of Christian reflection. When medieval Catholic thinkers insisted on a sharp distinction between "society" and the "state," they created a vaccine against absolutism in either its royal or modern (totalitarian) form. The vaccine wasn't completely effective. But its potency may help explain why the age of absolutism was a rather short one, as these things go in history.

Medieval Catholicism also helped plant in the Western mind the idea that "consent" is crucial to just governance. Government isn't simply coercion, medieval Catholic political theory insisted; just governance requires consent. Consent would be forthcoming if governance were just. And who would judge the justice of a particular form or style of governance, or the justice of a particular act of state? The Church's claim to be able to judge princes, and the Catholic teaching that "the people" have an inherent sense of justice within them, injected a crucial idea into the political-cultural subsoil of the West—the idea that "justice" isn't simply what those in authority say it is. There are moral standards of justice that are independent of governments; we can know those moral standards, and they ought to be applied in public life. All of these ideas, fundamental to democracy, were nurtured in the civilization of the Middle Ages by the Catholic Church.

Medieval Catholicism also taught lessons that are not so well remembered today—like the lesson that freedom is a matter of virtue, not just political mechanics. The idea that a free people must be a disciplined people, a people who nurture and cherish mastery of their passions, isn't exactly front and center in contemporary political theory. But it's part of the medieval heritage, along with these other proto-democratic ideas. Then there's the medieval idea that what we've come to call "rights" imply responsibilities. In a culture that often thinks of "rights" as free-floating claims to do whatever I like (so long as "no one else gets hurt"), that linkage between rights and responsibilities could stand some revisiting. Finally, we ought to reconsider what the medieval Church taught European culture about the "communitarian individual," in my friend Michael Novak's neat formulation. Yes, we're individuals who have ideas, create things, and enjoy inherent "rights." But none of that means much of anything without vibrant communities, whether that be family or professional group or guild or whatever. For an individual to grow into a truly human maturity requires a sense of responsibility for others, a commitment to working with others in society, and a sense of social solidarity. That's the "communitarian individual." A society that absolutizes the commons ends up crushing individual creativity and initiative. A society that absolutizes the individual will, sooner or later, comes apart at the seams. It's the old Catholic "both/and" again: *both* person *and* community, each affecting the other in important ways.

I'm not suggesting that the conventional story line on democracy is completely flawed. I am suggesting that it's incomplete. Yes, the Church, and particularly the papacy, accommodated itself to royal absolutism in Europe. Yes, several popes in the first two-thirds of the nineteenth century were deeply skeptical about democracy (in no small part because they identified "democracy" with what happened in France after 1789). And yes, the medieval Church learned a lot about the *res publica* from the Greeks (especially Aristotle). But the same medieval Church filtered that learning through its prior commitment to distinguishing the things of God from the things of Caesar. And the medieval Church embodied what it learned in a way of life that shaped the European culture that gave birth to modern democracy. The conventional story's suggestion that the roots of modern democracy go back no farther than the seventeenth (or possibly sixteenth) century makes no historical sense. Things just don't work that way.

John Carroll, working with Benjamin Latrobe to design the first Catholic cathedral in modernity's first democratic republic, understood that Catholics and their ideas weren't "foreign" to the American experience and experiment—no matter what the conventional story line said, and no matter what the bigots said. Catholics belonged in a democracy because the Catholic Church had formed the culture that, over time and under a welter of influences, eventually gave birth to the modern democratic project. That's why this building we're visiting deliberately evokes the spirit of the American founding *and* the spirit of the Great Tradition, formed in the West by the interaction of Jerusalem, Athens, and Rome. The two go together.

---

They're being torn apart today, though. And that brings us to the question of freedom, what it means, and what it's for.

Catholic thinking about freedom should begin where Catholic thinking about every other facet of the moral life begins—with the Beatitudes (Matthew 5:3–12). The Beatitudes are the basic gospel framework for thinking about the question, How should we live? Why? Because the Beatitudes point us to the eternal happiness for which the moral life, here and now, is a preparation. So here's another challenge to conventional wisdom: in the Catholic way of thinking, the moral life is not an arbitrary set of rules imposed on us by God and the Church. *The moral life involves rules for living that emerge from inside the human heart and its thirst for happiness with God.*

The basic moral question is not that familiar teenage query, How far can I go? The basic moral question is the adult question, What must I do to become a good person?—the kind of person who can actually enjoy living with God forever. In answering that question, we discover rules. But they emerge organically, not "from outside." They emerge from the dynamics of *becoming a good person*. That idea of the moral life—of a truly *human* life—leads to a very different idea of freedom.

If American popular and high culture could ever agree on a theme song that captures the idea of freedom driving much of contemporary life, it would almost certainly be Frank Sinatra's "My Way." *I did it my way* seems to sum up the widespread notion that freedom is a matter of asserting myself and my will—that freedom is really about *choice*, not about what we choose and why. Suggest that certain choices are incompatible with human dignity and with growth in goodness, and you'll get some very strange looks these days, on campus or in the workplace.

Catholicism has a different idea of freedom: freedom and goodness go together. A great contemporary moral theologian, Father Servais Pinckaers, O.P., explained all this through two brilliant metaphors. Learning to play the piano, he reminded us, is a tedious, even dreary business at first: well do I remember my own distaste for a book of technique-strengthening tortures entitled *Scales, Chords, and Arpeggios*. But after doing one's exercises for a while, what originally seemed like a burden comes into clearer focus—learning to do the right thing in the right way is actually liberating. You can play anything you like, even the most difficult pieces. You can make new music on your own. Sure, Father Pinckaers writes, anybody can pound away on a piano. But that's a "rudimentary, savage sort of freedom," not a truly human freedom. Do your exercises, master the art and discipline of playing the piano, and you discover a new and richer freedom—the freedom of doing the good things you want to do with perfection.

Then there's learning a new language. You've discovered, I'm sure, that the best way to learn a new language is to listen to it and speak it. At some point, though, we've got to learn grammar and vocabulary—the "rules" that turn noise into language. There's no communication without those rules; there's only gibberish. Father Pinckaers suggests that this common experience is really a window into the truth about freedom. Yes, language means living within a set of rules, but it's the rules that give me the freedom to make new sentences, to test new ideas, to communicate. To reduce freedom to the freedom to make mistakes demeans freedom and demeans us. Freedom involves learning to avoid mistakes without having to think about it. Freedom is doing the right thing and avoiding mistakes *by habit*. And another word for "habit" is *virtue*.

*I did it my way* teaches us an idea of freedom that Father Pinckaers calls "the freedom of indifference." Doing things "my way," just because it's *my* way, is like banging idiotically on the piano or talking gibberish. The richer, nobler idea of freedom the Catholic Church proposes is what Father Pinckaers calls *freedom for excellence*—the freedom to do the right thing in the right way for the right reasons—as a matter of habit. That's the truly human way. Because that's the kind of freedom that satisfies our natural desire for happiness, which itself reflects our desire for God, who is all Good, all the way.

Freedom helps us grow into the kind of people who can live with that God forever.

What's all this got to do with democracy? Everything.

Freedom untethered from moral truth will eventually become freedom's worst enemy. If there's only *your* truth and *my* truth and neither one of us acknowledges a transcendent referee—*the* truth—by which to settle our disagreements, then one of two things is going to happen: you're going to impose your power on me, or I'm going to impose my power on you. Persuasion, which is the life blood of democratic politics, gives way to coercion, which is an acid eating away at democratic institutions and commitments.

We're uncomfortably close to that situation in America today. Two generations of debonair nihilism have left us with a high culture, including the university world, in which two crucial ideas—that freedom has something to do with goodness and that goodness has something to do with fulfilling the noblest American aspirations to "equal justice for all"—are regarded as "medieval," laughable, even dangerous. That erosion of culture has, in turn, had a profound effect on our law.

When I was a boy, the U.S. Supreme Court ringingly affirmed the inclusion of all Americans in the community of common protection and concern in its epic 1954 *Brown v. Board of Education* decision, which outlawed segregation in government-supported schools. Less than forty years later, the Court was proposing a morally indifferent, content-free freedom as the official national creed of the United States, and indeed as the very purpose of American democracy. As three justices put it in 1992, writing in *Casey v. Planned Parenthood*, "At the heart of liberty is the right to define one's own concept of existence, of meaning, of the universe, and of the mystery of human life." A decade later, the Court drew on this bizarre "mystery passage" in its 2003 decision, *Lawrence v. Texas*, which suggests that the state's only interest in matters of human sexuality is protecting an unbridled license to fulfill what any configuration of consenting adults defines as personal "needs."

On this (mis)understanding of freedom, democracy is simply a set of procedures—electoral, legislative, judicial—by which "we the people" (or, more likely, they the courts) regulate the pursuit of personal satisfactions and pleasures. There's no moral core to democracy here. The Founders' "self-evident truths," which were *moral* truths, have disappeared into the ether. In this stripped-down, *I did it my way* vision of democracy, civil society is of no consequence. There's no great public moral argument about how we ought to live together, as people committed to freedom and to the truth about freedom. There are only The Rules of the Game, determined by either law or judicial fiat in order to leave unhampered my pursuit of the gratification of *me*—my willfulness, my self, indeed my selfishness.

The moral architecture of freedom in the United Sates is crumbling. Young Catholics have a real opportunity, and a great responsibility, to do something about that. You have to challenge the notion that, as three Supreme Court justices wrote a decade ago, linking freedom to moral truth through the law is an act of "compulsion" that denies our fellow citizens the "attributes of personhood." And the best way to challenge that notion of content-free democracy is to ask, What's the idea of *person* here? Isn't there something terribly demeaning about reducing the "attributes of personhood" to a bundle of undisciplined desires? Aren't we better than that?

Aren't we *more* than that? How are we going to have a genuine democracy if we can't talk with each other about what's good? How are we going to have a genuine democracy if, in the name of *I did it my way*, one class of citizens—who happen to be alive—asserts a "right" to take the lives of other indisputably human creatures, who happen not to have been born yet? How are we going to have a genuine democracy if the fit and healthy assert the "right" to dispose of the inconveniently elderly, terminally ill, or radically handicapped?

All of this is being asserted today in the name of a false idea of freedom. The best antidote to a bad idea is a good idea. That's your public job, as a young Catholic in the twenty-first century United States—to challenge the freedom of indifference with freedom for excellence. A lot depends on how well you do, including the question of whether twenty-first-century American democracy remains in any sense tethered to its founding principles.

John Carroll did not simply believe that Catholicism was "compatible" with democracy. Like other imaginative U.S. Catholic thinkers of his time and ours, he had the intuition that Catholic ideas about freedom just might be crucial to the future prosperity of the American democratic experiment. Could Carroll have foreseen our circumstances today? The idea's not as far-fetched as it might at first seem. Carroll had a very clear view of what the French Revolution—the world's first experiment in totalitarianism, an experiment based on radical assertions of willfulness—had done and meant. He knew, because he had seen, that democracy could degenerate into mobocracy or give birth to new and even bloodier forms of dictatorship if sufficient numbers of people bought a corrupt idea of freedom. I can't help but imagine that he had those ideas in the back of his mind when he helped Latrobe design this magnificent building. The roots of democracy run more deeply into our civilizational soil than some suspect. This building, in which the heritage of that civilization met the bright new promise of a democratic future, reminds us that Catholics in the United States have a special responsibility for tending to democracy's deepest roots.

I hope that you, and others like you, will be skillful and dedicated gardeners of freedom.

## 14

## The Basilica of the Holy Trinity, Kraków—On Not Being Alone

The Dominican Basilica of the Holy Trinity in Kraków is only a few hundred yards from the Rynek Głowny, the Old Town market square. Like a lot of Kraków, the city's Dominican priory is thick with history. St. Hyacinth (c. 1200–1257) is buried in the basilica. Hyacinth (or Jacek, as he's known here) brought his friend Dominic's new Order of Friars Preachers to Poland in the early thirteenth century and persuaded his kinsman, Iwo Odrowąż, bishop of Kraków, to give the Dominicans this property as their Polish base of operations. The basilica itself dates from the latter part of the thirteenth century; the steeply gabled front, its most striking design feature, was an addition in 1462. Tomas Torquemada, the feared Inquisitor, once stayed here. The interior was gutted by a fire in 1850; rather than redecorate in the art nouveau style, as the neighboring Franciscans had done in restoring their fire-damaged basilica, the Dominicans chose a modified Gothic style, so you can actually get a sense of what a medieval cathedral looked like, especially as you look up from the nave at the blue ceiling with its delicate net vaulting. During the Second World War, the Nazis shut down the high school the Dominicans ran on the priory property and used the school yard as a supply depot. Some of the older Fathers will tell you today that, as young men in the 1940s, they'd sneak out into the yard at night, "appropriate" foodstuffs for the starving citizens of Kraków, and then fill the bottom third of the shipping canisters with rocks—"And that's why the Germans lost in Russia!"

When I first came to Kraków in 1991, the basilica was almost black, from centuries of coal dust and decades of communist-era neglect. Ten years of cleaning and restoration have brought back to glowing life the different red hues of the medieval brick, as well as the decorative stone bosses on the gabled facade. Marvelous funerary monuments have been restored along the four walls of the priory's former cloister; this vaulted walkway, where you can often find art students sketching, opens on one side into a fine chapter house, beneath which are buried the bones of eight centuries of Polish Dominicans. When Pope John Paul II came to the basilica in June 1999 to venerate the relics of St. Hyacinth and greet Poland's Dominican priests, brothers, and nuns, the provincial, Father Maciej Zięba, welcomed him with the words, "Holy Father, Polish Dominicans have been waiting for this moment for 777 years." I've gotten to know the place well during numerous visits. The priory was my Kraków base when I was researching John Paul's biography; I've taught here every summer since 1994 in a seminar on Catholic social doctrine for students from the new democracies of east central Europe and North America; many of the fathers and student brothers are good friends in that remarkable extended family that's the Catholic Church.

The best time to come to the basilica is at 7:00 P.M. on a Sunday night—not because it's quiet then but because it isn't. The Dominicans run a vibrant chaplaincy to students at the nearby Jagiellonian University, and the 7:00 P.M. Mass every Sunday is for them. I was here, for example, on June 29, 2003, the Sunday after the university finished its spring semester. Despite the exodus from the university the previous week, the basilica was completely packed, as it is every Sunday at 7:00 P.M., with almost three thousand young people. They're everywhere—in the pews, on folding chairs, in the old monastic choir stalls, perched on the great marble stairway leading up to the tomb of St. Hyacinth, sitting on the steps of the wooden Gothic confessionals, spilling out into the street. There's nothing fancy about their dress, which is in the universal student mode: jeans and T-shirts are ubiquitous. The choir—all students—is wonderful, blending traditional Gregorian and Polish chants and hymns with more contemporary music from the ecumenical monastery at Taizé in France. The preaching is intellectually and morally demanding, but it's also punctuated with wry humor. Altogether, it's a very, very impressive liturgical experience.

My hunch is that the beauty of the liturgy won't be your most enduring memory of 7:00 P.M. Sunday night Mass at the Dominican basilica in Kraków, though. What will stick in your mind's eye are the faces—for that's what everyone I bring here seems to remember most vividly. They're intense and relaxed at the same time. They're the faces of people who know that in coming to *this* place, they've come into one of those borderlands between the human and the divine that we've been discussing. Young men and women don't look like this when they're coming to Mass primarily to obey the rules and keep their parents happy. People look like this when they're *convicted*, as an evangelical Protestant from the Deep South might say. As one friend put it after his first experience of the 7:00 P.M. Mass, these young people participate in the liturgy and listen to Scripture and preaching, "as if their lives depended on it."

Which, of course, they do. That's why those three thousand young adults know something that the conventional wisdom hasn't figured out yet—or, perhaps better, doesn't want to admit. And that "something" is worth thinking about.

---

According to the conventional story line of modernity, "modernization" means secularization—the withering away of traditional religious belief and practice. On this reading of things, "modernity" and "religion" are a zero-sum game: the more modern you are, the less religious you become; and the more religious you are, the less susceptible you are to modernization. At the beginning of the twentieth century, advanced thinkers widely predicted that the new century then unfolding would witness a maturing humanity, tutored by science, lose its "need" for religion. Religious belief and practice were for children, perhaps adolescents. A mature, adult humanity had no "need" of God.

We've already talked about what happened when those predictions held true—great swaths of the world were turned into an abattoir *in the name of humanism*. In the 1940s, the French theologian Henri de Lubac, who would later become an influential figure at the Second

Vatican Council, tried to parse this strange, lethal phenomenon, which he called "atheistic humanism." Atheism, of course, was nothing new; the village atheist and the radically skeptical intellectual had long been stock figures in the human drama. *Atheistic humanism* was something altogether different, Father de Lubac suggested. This wasn't a matter of skeptical individuals scratching their particular itches to discomfort the neighbors or impress the faculty tenure committee. This was atheism with a developed ideology and a program for remaking the world. And its prophets—prominent among them Comte, Feuerbach, Marx, and Nietszche—all taught that the God of the Bible was an enemy of human dignity.

Now *that*, de Lubac argued, was a great reversal. Look at the difference between the classical world—embodied in, say, the *Iliad* and the *Odyssey*—and the biblical world. In the *Iliad* and the *Odyssey*, even the greatest mortals are subjected to the whims of the (usually frivolous or mean-spirited) gods. Things are very different in the Bible. Biblical religion—the revelation of the God of Abraham, Isaac, Jacob, Moses, and Jesus—was a tremendous liberation from the whims of the gods or the workings-out of Fate. As Father de Lubac put it, if God had created the world and the men and women in it, and if every human being had a direct link to the Creator through worship and prayer, then men and women were no longer playthings; they were free, and they were responsible. The God of the Bible was not a willful tyrant. Nor was he a remote abstraction. Nor was he a cosmic watchmaker, content to create the world, wind it up, and then leave it to its own devices. The God of Abraham, Isaac, Jacob, Moses, and Jesus entered history and had become our companion on the pilgrimage of life. To be in communion with this

God was to be liberated from Fate, liberated for freedom, liberated for human excellence.

The phenomenon that Henri de Lubac called "atheistic humanism" turned this upside down and inside out. What Judaism and Christianity proposed as liberation, atheistic humanism called bondage. Which meant, in turn, that jettisoning God was the precondition to human greatness. This was neither the atheism of the intellectually fashionable nor the atheism of despair. This was atheistic *humanism*, on the march in the name of human liberation. And this new idea, de Lubac proposed, had the gravest consequences. Brought into action by the great tyrants of the mid-twentieth century, this new thing proved something that you and the members of your generation should reflect very carefully. It was once said, Father de Lubac recalled, that men couldn't organize the world without God. That, in fact, is not true; atheistic humanism disproved that claim. What atheistic humanism had also proven, however, was that without God, human beings could only organize the world against each other. Ultramundane humanism, de Lubac concluded, is inevitably *inhuman* humanism, even if it imagines itself to be motivated by the highest intentions.

If this business of "atheistic humanism" seems familiar, it's because it's the intellectual broth in which you've been simmering for most of your life. The roughest edges, to put it gently, have been ground off the project of atheistic humanism—although it took a world war and a Cold War to finish Nazism and communism, the two most lethal expressions of this misbegotten creed. But residues remain: in the positivism Western high culture learned from Comte, the subjectivism it learned from Feuerbach, the materialism it learned from Marx, the radical willfulness it learned from Nietzsche—and in the assumption that biblical religion is for children. The immature. The psychologically "needy." Our old friend John Henry Newman once wrote that genuine university life would be impossible without serious theology because genuine intellectual life is impossible without theology. I doubt you'll find that claim seriously in play at any of the prestige schools that *U.S. News and World Report* ranks every fall. On the contrary—that human maturity requires "liberation" from biblical religion and its demands is as firm an orthodoxy as you'll find on many American campuses and in many American graduate schools today.

At least among the faculty. Students today are different. I meet thousands of university and graduate students every year; most of them have never heard of Henri de Lubac. But I think they'd be sympathetic to his analysis because of conclusions they've reached on their own: bad ideas have bad consequences, atheistic humanism is a bad idea, and the softer forms of atheistic humanism that shaped and misshaped (and in some cases wrecked) their parents' lives are ideas to be avoided. Young people today are open to biblical religion and its understanding of the human condition in ways that were difficult to imagine twenty-five, or even fifteen, years ago. It's the professoriate that's locked into the past.

I thought of these young people, their questions and their quandaries, when I was in Germany in October 2002. In front of the Catholic archdiocesan offices in Cologne is a striking bronze memorial to Edith Stein, St. Teresa Benedicta of the Cross, whom I've mentioned before—the distinguished philosopher and Carmelite nun who was martyred in Auschwitz in 1942. There are actually three lifesized Edith Steins clustered in the memorial. The first is a young Jewish girl, holding the Star of David, thinking about the God of Israel, beginning to experience skepticism about her ancestral faith. The second Edith Stein is the rising star of modern German philosophy, more determined in visage but with a split head (remarkably composed by the sculptor); faith and reason haven't been put back together, and neither has the life of Edith Stein. The third Edith Stein in the memorial is the Carmelite-and-philosopher who has found the reconciliation of faith and reason—and the integration of her own life—in Jesus Christ. This Edith Stein, Sister Teresa "Blessed by the Cross," holds that cross in front of her as she sets out on the pathway that leads to the ultimate gift of self. The third Edith Stein is the whole Edith Stein. And that wholeness is what I sense young people looking for today, in a culture that tends to pull us apart (as it had once done to Edith Stein).

The story of Edith Stein suggests that the alternative to ultramundane humanism and the antidote to its lethal effects isn't to abandon the great project of western humanism; *the alternative is Christian humanism, a humanism built on the three theological virtues of faith, hope, and love.* That's the truth and the love that seized Edith Stein and made her whole. That's what so many young people are looking for today—a humanism that is truly humanizing and humane. You can find that humanity and that wholeness in Christ. I'd guess that not many of those thousands of young people at the 7:00 P.M. Mass at the Dominican basilica in Kraków have ever studied Reinhold Niebuhr, who was a great preacher, if not exactly a great theologian, when he dominated one wing of American Protestantism in the mid-twentieth century. But they've sensed the truth of what Niebuhr once described as the effects of faith, hope, and love in our lives:

> *Nothing that is worth doing can be achieved in our lifetime; therefore we must be saved by hope. Nothing which is true or beautiful or good makes complete sense in any immediate context of history; therefore we must be saved by faith. Nothing we do, however virtuous, can be accomplished alone; therefore we are saved by love. No virtuous act is quite as virtuous from the standpoint of our friend or foe as it is from our standpoint. Therefore we must be saved by the final form of love which is forgiveness.*

---

The twenty-first-century world is not becoming more secular. In that sense, the "secularization hypothesis"—that modernization inevitably leads to secularization—has been falsified. For better and for worse, the world of this new century and new millennium is becoming more intensely religious. As my friend Peter Berger, the eminent sociologist of religion, has tirelessly pointed out for years, what needs explaining is not the endurance and tenacity of religious belief; what needs explaining are those bunkers of secularism that still dominate our high culture. India doesn't need explaining (although it certainly needs to be understood). The 7:00 P.M. Mass at the Dominicans in Kraków doesn't need explaining. The waves of pilgrims at the shrine of Our Lady of Guadalupe in Mexico City don't need explaining. What needs explaining are the Princeton faculty club, the Harvard Law School faculty, French politicians, and several members of the U.S. Supreme Court.

As journalist David Brooks has pointed out, that's the first step in "recovering" from the habit of secularism, or perhaps better, the habit of taking the secularization hypothesis seriously: to recognize that, as a religious person, *you're not alone*. And you're not . . . odd. The real minority, Brooks argues, are those "pockets of people in the world who do not feel the constant presence of God in their lives, who do not fill their days with rituals and prayers and garments that bring them into contact with the divine, and who do not believe that God's will should shape their public lives."

Brooks was writing for what he calls "recovering secularists," but his advice holds true for religious people who get spooked by the dominance of the secularists in our high culture. Perhaps his wisest counsel involves a question of nerve and historical perspective—if it's true that the world is becoming more, not less, religious, doesn't that mean that the world is becoming a much more dangerous place? Maybe the secularists were right on this point, at least; maybe a thoroughly secularized politics is the safest politics. But they're not right on this, as Henri de Lubac knew. The greatest slaughters of the twentieth century were not perpetrated by religions but by atheistic humanism. Yes, there are competing visions of human destiny at work in the world, many of them religiously informed, and some of them volatile. But that's history. That's humanity. That's the way things were, are, and always will be. "Beating the secularist prejudices out of our minds every day" is, David Brooks suggests, an essential part of trying to push history in a more humane direction. It's certainly essential in engaging those parts of the Islamic world who reject the warped marriage of a distorted form of Islam and Western nihilism that creates the terrorism of al Qaeda, the Taliban, and all the rest. If, as secularists seem to suggest, engaging the Islamic world means turning "moderate" Muslims into good Western secularizing liberals, then we really are condemned to a bloody clash of civilizations.

Keeping our nerve also means recognizing that, if I may borrow a splendid trope from Ben Wattenberg, the good news is that the bad news isn't all the news there is. Penn State historian Philip Jenkins has painted a vivid portrait of the "next Christendom" in a book by that title. Yes, on the current form sheet, western Europe, Canada, Australia, and New Zealand seem thoroughly secularized and unlikely to recover their Christian roots anytime soon. But they're the historical aberrations, not the norm.

Various expressions of Protestant Christianity are flourishing in Latin America and Africa, often in unexpected forms; on the numbers here, Jenkins suggests, Pentecostalism is the most successful social movement of the past century. At the same time, the Catholicism in which you'll spend your life is also "moving south"—of the equator. By 2025, Jenkins estimates, almost three-quarters of world Catholicism will be found in Africa, Asia, and Latin America. Latin America is already world Catholicism's demographic center of gravity. The dialogue about what it means to be "the Church in the modern world" between the vibrant if troubled Catholic Church in the United States and the Church in Latin America is going to be arguably the most important Catholic conversation of the twenty-first century. Then there is African Catholicism, which is exploding with energy and astonishing growth. In the early 1950s, there were 16 million Catholics in Africa; there are 120 million African Catholics today and there may be as many as 240 million African Catholics by 2050.

These new Catholics live a Christianity that Jenkins describes as very close to the New Testament in its sensibility: the supernatural is as real as the natural world, Jesus embodies a divine power to heal the wounds of life, authority is respected, and no one is clamoring for a "democratized" Church (whatever that would mean). Might you see the day, sometime in the mid to late twenty-first century, when African missionaries reevangelize the old Catholic heartland of western Europe? Will the foundations for that reevangelization be laid in the first half of the new century by some of those Poles you met at the 7:00 P.M. Dominican Mass in Kraków? It's not impossible; about one-third of all European seminarians today are in Poland. Properly formed and trained, they could become a remarkably potent force for the reevangelization of the "Old Europe," in cooperation with the lay renewal movements—often led by young people—that are some of the liveliest parts of Catholicism in France, Germany, Italy, and Spain.

So you're not alone, as a young religious believer and a young Catholic. And you're not on the back side of history. You're on its cutting edge.

---

Twenty-five years ago, if anyone had suggested that rallies of millions of young people would become one of the signature events of the Catholic Church around the world, secularists would have scoffed—and so would a lot of Catholics, including senior clergymen. Pope John Paul II had a different view. Having spent much of his ministry as a young priest with young people, he believed that the next generation of Catholics was just waiting to be rallied. So he decided to rally them.

The results have been the remarkable World Youth Days of the past two decades—Rome, 1985; Buenos Aires, 1987; Santiago de Compostela, 1989; Częstochowa, 1991; Denver, 1993; Manila, 1995; Paris, 1997; Rome again, for the Great Jubilee of 2000; Toronto, 2002. Each of these events had its own special character, but each had a similar liturgical rhythm.

World Youth Days are meant to re-create the experience of Holy Week, which is both the center of the Church's year of grace and the basic structure of the spiritual life. Thus every World Youth Day begins with a variant on Palm Sunday, during which the large "World Youth Day cross," which has been carried around the host country for months, is solemnly processed into the site of the opening ceremony. Then there is the analogue to Holy Thursday, during which the Pope discusses living a life of gospel service. Every World Youth Day then has its "Good Friday," in which young Catholics and the Pope pray together over man's redemption through the enduring mystery of the cross. The following night there's an evening candlelit vigil service, analogous to the Great Vigil of Easter on Holy Saturday evening. Every World Youth Day ends with a Mass that evokes the experience of Easter Sunday and sends everyone back out into the world with the message of the resurrection.

I think the most memorable moment of World Youth Day 1997 in Paris was the vigil. For three days, the half million young pilgrims had been scattered in several dozen different venues throughout Paris. Now, for the vigil, they all came to the Longchamp racecourse, filling the infield and surrounding area. The racecourse was turned into a cathedral of light, as the Pope baptized twelve young adults, drawn from every continent. The

French, dumbfounded at the turnout, watched this extraordinary demonstration of faith with amazement. The next night, on French national TV, Cardinal Jean-Marie Lustiger of Paris drove the message home in an interview with a shocked anchorman who couldn't understand what all of this was about. It was a question of generations, the cardinal suggested to his skeptical questioner. The anchorman belonged to a generation that had been raised Catholic, lost its faith somewhere around 1968, and had been fighting daddy, as it were, ever since. *This* generation was different, the cardinal insisted. "They grew up with nothing. They have found Jesus Christ. They want to explore all that that means." These young people, in other words, hadn't bought the conventional story line. The anchorman was the one in a time warp.

In Toronto in 2002, it was the Good Friday analogue that made the greatest impact on me, and I expect on many others. Toronto is a self-consciously secular city, priding itself on a "tolerance" and "diversity" that often seem to have room for everything except culturally assertive Christian conviction. Yet on the night of July 26, 2002, Toronto saw something its secularist establishment hadn't imagined possible—half a million young people making their way up University Avenue from the business district to the provincial parliament buildings and Queen's Park, devoutly praying the Way of the Cross. The Canadian Broadcasting Corporation estimated that as many as 1 billion people around the world shared that extraordinary moment, thanks to real-time television hookups to 160 countries. But I doubt the impact anywhere was greater than in securely secular Toronto itself.

The remaining skeptics continue to suggest that World Youth Days are simply a variant on contemporary youth culture's infatuation with celebrity—in this case, the Pope. No one who ever attended one of these events could say that, I don't think. In his eighth and ninth decades, and as physical infirmities slowed him down, the Pope had long since transcended the "John Paul Superstar" phase of his pontificate. And in any case, at what other festival on the world youth circuit are young people challenged to lead lives of moral heroism?

During World Youth Day 2000 in Rome, the more aggressively secular Italian media contrasted the "Rome people" with the "Rimini people"—the latter being the hundreds of thousands of youngsters flocking to Italy's beaches in August—and asked what the difference was between the two groups. Surely both had a claim to defining the European future, the papers suggested. But that's hardly the point, is it? The question is what future is being defined, and whether there's any place for a call to spiritual grandeur and moral heroism in that future. Western Europe's catastrophically low birth rates demonstrate that two generations of Europeans have failed to create a future in the most elemental human sense—by creating a successor generation capable of sustaining society. It's hard to imagine that that phenomenon doesn't have anything to do with the corrosive effects of the acids of skepticism, moral relativism, and what I once called in these letters "debonair nihilism." That so many young people are at least intrigued by John Paul II's call to hold the bar of spiritual and moral expectation high and to live the Law of the Gift written on their hearts shouldn't be considered a threat to Europe's future, or anywhere else's. In some cases, that kind of conversion may be the precondition to any future at all.

---

By all means put a future World Youth Day on your schedule; the next one is scheduled for Cologne in 2005. World Youth Days sum up, somehow, many of the subjects we've considered in these letters: why deciding on your "vocation," that unique something that only you can be and do, is so important a part of becoming an adult Catholic; why stuff counts; why the real world is the world of transcendent truth and love, revealed in and through the things of this world; why "putting on" the sacramental imagination is part of becoming the fully human being you want to be. World Youth Days offer a great experience of Catholic solidarity and Catholic enthusiasm. They're also great experiences of sacramentality. Here you can see, hear, touch, feel, and taste that, in the Catholic view of things, we meet God through visible, tangible, audible things—including the Church itself and the sacraments the Church makes available to us.

This distinctive Catholic worldliness is ever more important in a world that, by taking itself with ultimate seriousness, doesn't take itself seriously enough. Taking the world seriously doesn't mean falling into the trap of materialism and skepticism. Taking the world seriously means taking the world for what it is—the arena of God's action, the place where we meet the love that satisfies our yearning for a love that satisfies absolutely and without reservation.

Welcome to the real world.

# Sources

## Letter One

Flannery O'Connor citations are from *The Habit of Being: Letters of Flannery O'Connor*, ed. Sally Fitzgerald (New York: Farrar, Straus, Giroux, 1979).

## Letter Two

John E. Walsh's 1982 book, *The Bones of St. Peter: The Fascinating Account of the Search for the Apostle's Body*, is available through Catholic bookstores or online book services. The citations from Flannery O'Connor are from *The Habit of Being*.

There's a wonderful story about the obelisk in St. Peter's Square that fits better here than in the letter. The obelisk remained in place, to the left of the current St. Peter's, for centuries. When Sixtus V ordered his architect, Domenico Fontana, to move the obelisk to the center of the square, Fontana had a problem: no one knew how to do this. Nine hundred men, 150 horses, and 47 cranes were in the square on September 18, 1586, to try to move and then reerect the obelisk without damaging it. Sixtus ordered that the procedure be carried out in complete silence to avoid spooking the horses—and to underscore the point, he had a gallows erected in the square, on which anyone who made a noise would be summarily hung. As the ropes began to pull the obelisk upright, they became so taut that they began to smolder; yet no one dared to breathe a word until finally a sailor cried, *Acqua alle funi!* ("Water on the ropes!"), thus saving the day and the obelisk. Pope Sixtus was so grateful to have been disobeyed that he gave the sailor's hometown, Bordighera, the privilege of providing palms for the Palm Sunday service at St. Peter's—a tradition which continues to this day.

### Letter Three

Citations from Jaroslav Pelikan are from *Jesus Through the Centuries: His Place in the History of Culture* (New Haven: Yale University Press, 1985).

The Waugh biography cited is Martin Stannard, *Evelyn Waugh: The Later Years, 1939–1966* (New York: Norton, 1992).

Waugh's letter to George Orwell is in *The Letters of Evelyn Waugh*, ed. Mark Amory (New York: Penguin, 1980).

Hans Urs von Balthasar's description of Catholicism as God's search for us is taken from Balthasar, *In the Fullness of Faith: On the Centrality of the Distinctively Catholic* (San Francisco: Ignatius, 1988).

### Letter Four

Pope John Paul II's vocational memoir is *Gift and Mystery: On the Fiftieth Anniversary of My Priestly Ordination* (New York: Doubleday, 1996).

Hans Urs von Balthasar's analysis of the different images or profiles shaping the Church in every age is in *The Office of Peter and the Structure of the Church* (San Francisco: Ignatius, 1986).

## Letter Five

Newman's Roman address in 1879 is cited in Ian Ker, *John Henry Newman: A Biography* (New York: Oxford University Press, 1988).

The story of Edith Stein's conversion may be found in Freda Mary Oben, *Edith Stein: Scholar, Feminist, Saint* (New York: Alba House, 1988).

David Gelernter's description of "ice-your-own-cupcake" religion is in the September 2003 issue of *Commentary*.

The citation from Newman's *Loss and Gain* is from Avery Cardinal Dulles, S.J., *Newman* (New York: Continuum, 2002).

The text of the Hartford Appeal is in *Against the World For the World: The Hartford Appeal and the Future of American Religion*, ed. Peter L. Berger and Richard John Neuhaus (New York: Seabury, 1976).

## Letter Six

Joseph Pearce's biography of Belloc is *Old Thunder: A Life of Hilaire Belloc* (San Francisco: Ignatius, 2002).

The citations from G.K. Chesterton's *Orthodoxy* are from the Image Books edition (Garden City, N.Y.: Doubleday Image, 1959).

Chesterton's introduction to Aquinas is found in *St. Thomas Aquinas/St. Francis of Assisi* (San Francisco: Ignatius, 2002).

Gerard Manley Hopkins's poem "Pied Beauty" is taken from *Hopkins: Poems and Prose* (London: Penguin, 1963).

## Letter Seven

Evelyn Waugh's August 9, 1955, letter to Edith Sitwell is included in *The Letters of Evelyn Waugh.*

The citations from *Brideshead Revisited* are from the Penguin classics edition (London: Penguin, 2000).

Douglas Lane Patey's biography of Waugh is *The Life of Evelyn Waugh: A Critical Biography* (Oxford: Blackwell, 1998).

C. S. Lewis's reference to heaven as an "acquired taste" is from the introduction to Dorothy L. Sayers's translation of Dante's *Paradiso* (London: Penguin, 1962).

The citations from Robert Bolt's *A Man for All Seasons* are from the Vintage Books edition (New York: Vintage, 1962).

## Letter Eight

H. V. Morton's *A Traveler in Rome* has recently been reprinted by DaCapo Press and the citation is from that 2002 edition.

The "theology of the body" is outlined in greater detail in my *Witness to Hope: The Biography of Pope John Paul II* (New York: HarperCollins, 1999). For a more detailed exposition, see Christopher West, *Theology of the Body Explained* (Boston: Pauline Books and Media, 2003). The 129 original texts of John Paul's "theology of the body" audience addresses are also published in a one-volume edition by Pauline Books and Media.

## Letter Nine

Further information on St. Mary's Parish in Greenville, South Carolina, may be obtained by visiting the parish's Web site, www.stmarysgvl.org.

The Second Vatican Council's description of the Church's liturgy as a participation in the heavenly liturgy may be found in *Sacrosanctum Concilium*, "Dogmatic Constitution on the Liturgy," 8.

The texts from the *Catechism of the Catholic Church* are found at no. 2460.

## Letter Ten

Michael Kaufman's description of the Mass for the Fatherland is taken from his book *Mad Dreams, Saving Graces: Poland—A Nation in Conspiracy* (New York: Random House, 1989).

Hans Urs von Balthasar's description of some saints as "God's prime numbers" is taken from the introduction to his book, *Two Sisters in the Spirit* (San Francisco: Ignatius, 1992).

The Dawson citation is from Christopher Dawson, *Religion and the Rise of Western Culture* (New York: Doubleday Image, 1991).

John Paul II's reflections on his vocational struggles are found in *Gift and Mystery.*

**Letter Eleven**

Hans Urs von Balthasar's description of the cross is taken from *The Threefold Garland: The World's Salvation in Mary's Prayer* (San Francisco: Ignatius, 1982).

Peter Kreeft's reflections on suffering are in *Making Sense Out of Suffering* (Ann Arbor, Mich.: Servant, 1986).

Leon Kass's essay, "L'Chaim and Its Limits," is in the May 2001 issue of *First Things.*

**Letter Twelve**

Malcolm Miller's incomparable guide to Chartres is *Chartres Cathedral* (Andover, U.K.: Jarrold, 1996).

Hans Urs von Balthasar's analysis of the "genius" of art and what it teaches us about God may be found in *The Glory of the Lord: A Theological Aesthetics*, vol. 1, *Seeing the Form* (San Francisco: Ignatius, 1982).

Augustine's "Late have I loved thee" is from Book 10: xxvii (38) of the *Confessions.*

Cardinal Schönborn's analysis of icons may be found in Christoph Schönborn, *God's Human Face: The Christ-Icon* (San Francisco: Ignatius, 1994).

**Letter Thirteen**

Information on the Old Cathedral in Baltimore may be found at www.baltimorebasilica.org.

The contributions of medieval Catholic thought and life to modern democracy are outlined in John Courtney Murray, S.J., *We Hold These Truths: Catholic Reflections on the American Proposition* (Garden City, N.Y.: Doubleday Image, 1964).

Father Servais Pinckaers's distinction between the "freedom of indifference" and "freedom for excellence" is taken from his book, *The Sources of Christian Ethics* (Washington: Catholic University of America Press, 1995).

The Supreme Court's "mystery passage" is found in the 1992 case, *Casey v. Planned Parenthood*, 112 S. Ct. 2791, at 2807.

**Letter Fourteen**

Henri de Lubac's study, *The Drama of Atheist Humanism*, is published by San Francisco's Ignatius Press.

Reinhold Niebuhr's thoughts on faith, hope, love, and forgiveness are cited by Wilfred McClay in his essay, "The New Irony of American History," *First Things*, February 2002.

David Brooks's article, "Kicking the Secularist Habit: A Six-Step Program," was published in the March 2003 issue of *Atlantic*.

Philip Jenkins's book, *The Next Christendom: The Coming of Global Christianity*, was published by Oxford University Press in 2002.

# Acknowledgments

Elizabeth Maguire, publisher of Basic Books, urged me to write these letters. I thank her for her persistence, persuasiveness, and thoughtful editorial counsel. Thanks, too, to my agent, Loretta Barrett, for helping convince me that there was a there there.

Carrie Gress and Joan Weigel read the manuscript with care and made many useful suggestions.

For help with materials, reminiscences, contacts, references, and revisions I should like to thank Father Peter Cameron, O.P., Father Derek Cross, Father J. Scott Duarte, Dr. Henry T. Edmondson III, Father Zbigniew Krysiewicz, O.P., Father Roger Landry, Piotr and Teresa Malecki, Father Michael McGarry, C.S.P., Father Christopher Nalty, Father Guy Nicholls, Father Jay Scott Newman, Joseph Pearce, George Cardinal Pell, Mark Potter, Dr. Manfred Spieker, Jack Valero, and Father Maciej Zięba, O.P.. Avery Cardinal Dulles, S.J., Father William Joensen, Leon Kass, M.D., Father Richard John Neuhaus, Father Edward Oakes, S.J., and Dr. Douglas Lane Patey will all find here echoes of our conversations, for which I am grateful.

For the past twelve summers I've had the privilege of teaching young Catholics from North America and the new democracies of central and eastern Europe in the Tertio Millennio Seminar on the Free Society, which met in Liechtenstein in 1992–1993 and has met every summer since in Kraków. Our students have come from Belarus, Bulgaria, Canada, the Czech Republic, Hungary, Italy, Latvia, Lithuania, Moldova, Poland, Romania, Russia, Slovakia, Slovenia, Ukraine, and the United States. Many of them will do great things for the Church and the world in the future; others are already doing so. I'm grateful for the inspiration they've been to me and I'm happy to be able to dedicate this book to all of them.

*G.W.*
*October 19, 2003*
*Commemoration of the North American Martyrs*

## About the Author

George Weigel, a Roman Catholic theologian and one of the world's leading authorities on the Catholic Church, is the author of the acclaimed international bestseller, *Witness to Hope: The Biography of John Paul II*, as well as *The Truth of Catholicism*, *The Final Revolution*, and *The Courage To Be Catholic*. Now a senior fellow of the Ethics and Public Policy Center in Washington, D.C., where he holds the John M. Olin Chair in Religion and American Democracy, Weigel writes a weekly column, "The Catholic Difference," that is syndicated throughout the United States. He is an NBC consultant on Vatican affairs and appears regularly on network and cable television programs as well as on radio. Weigel lives with his wife and their three children in North Bethesda, Maryland.